Dressing your Personal Brand

The ultimate guide to leveraging your appearance to be happier, more successful, and less stressed

"Life isn't about finding yourself.
Life is about creating yourself."

- George Bernard Shaw

Table of Contents

Introduction

WHY IT MATTERS

Every time I talk to college students about personal branding and why their appearance matters, there is always a student who speaks up and says something to this effect:

But, Ms. Friedman, I should be judged by the quality of my work and how well I do in my classes, NOT by what I look like!

If you share this mind set, congratulations! Your parents have done a fine job raising you to be a hardworking and career driven (albeit a tad idealistic) individual. What they forgot to mention, however, is that sheer hard work and intelligence can only get you so far. No matter how smart you are, if you don't look presentable, you will most likely never earn that big time role representing your company.

So, unless you are the next Albert Einstein or some equivocal prodigal genius, listen up to this very important truth:

You can't change the fact that people will judge you, but you can control the judgements that are made.

Did you get that? Everyone you encounter on a daily basis, from your spouse in the morning to the CEO in your office hallway, makes mental judgements about you. It's not good or bad, it's just what we do as people. We are trained to look at our environment and make observations; it's part of our animalistic nature that helped to keep us alive in cavemen times. Just as smaller animals steer clear of larger hungry looking animals, we tend to judge people as a means to keep ourselves safe. Do you change directions when that rough looking, intoxicated man comes stumbling out of the bar in your direction? Of course you do. That's just you making innate judgements to help keep yourself safe. While not everyone that looks 'rough' is a threat, we still tend to make snap judgements. We aren't at risk of getting eaten by wild animals anymore, but our brain still takes observations of our surroundings and processes them through the filter of our culture. That is what leads the CEO to look at you and think, "Why does that slob work at my company?" or "I'm glad such a pulled together person is representing my company."

Even though the reality of being judged because of brain hardwiring seems a bit depressing, it shouldn't. Ever the optimist, I'm going to employ my favorite (and perhaps, to some people, most annoying) phrase here: look at the opportunity! I mean really, just look at the opportunity! We have a situation where you know something (in this case: judgement) is going to take place AND we have the opportunity to alter the results in our favor. Simply by altering our appearance, we can lead others to believe certain things about ourselves. We, essentially, have near complete control over how others perceive us. Isn't that exciting?

Now, I want you to imagine your ultimate woman crush (or man crush, if you are a man). It could be someone from the past like Audrey Hepburn, Elizabeth Taylor, or Jacqueline Onassis Kennedy. It could be someone who is currently living such as Oprah, Ellen, or Kelly Ripa. Whoever you decide, ask yourself what you love most about this person. Do you find her undeniably classy, graceful, and refined? Maybe you love how fun, energetic, and progressive she is. Chances are, you aren't the only person that thinks those things about your particular crush. There's a reason each of those public figures are dotted over: they have successfully figured out what makes them unique and then made a conscious and consistent effort to display those defining characteristics that they wish to be known for, through every part of their life. They act, dress, and live a certain way because a) it is ultimately in their nature to do so and b) that is how they want to be perceived. These icons have effectively taken advantage of the fact that people judge and have altered their own destinies.

It's great to have strong women or men as a source of inspiration, but it's even better to become your own muse. Throughout this book, you will learn to love yourself, dress yourself, and live the life you've always wanted. After all, the choice is yours, and oh just look at the opportunity!

Chapter 1:
Embrace the Power of Personal Branding

WHAT EXACTLY *IS* PERSONAL BRANDING?

In 1997, Tom Peters wrote a revolutionary article in Fast Company magazine titled, "The Brand Called You". His radically new concept of personal branding was exciting to few and forgotten by many. Fast forward ten years and those excited few, who understood where our culture was going, took the concept and ran with it. They became hugely influential and successful in the field of personal branding and were followed by many others eager to break into the industry. Now you have hundreds of personal branding gurus who seek to help you stand out in a world that is ever changing.

What those gurus understand is this: The workplace is moving away from a one size fits all. More qualified candidates are available in your industry than ever before and competition is stiff. However, they also know that you have unique accomplishments, attributes, and characteristics that set you apart from others in your career field and personal life. By embracing those attributes, you can not only make it through this workplace shift, but come out on top. Essentially, your personal brand is the combination of attributes and accomplishments that define you and set you apart from others.

The whole concept of personal branding is a bit abstract, so I like to make it more relatable by talking about cookies. (I also just like talking about cookies.) Take Oreos for instance. I say Oreo and you instantly have a few ideas in mind. Most of us conjure up mental images of two little black cookies with crème sandwiched in between. We may think about milk, the iconic blue packaging, or even recall an Oreo related memory from childhood. This didn't happen by coincidence; the Nabisco brand has worked hard for years to create a strong brand around Oreo. They have intentionally created marketing that would result in you making the previously stated associations. They started by deciding what kind of cookies they would make and what their main characteristics would be. In this case, it would be two chocolate cookies with a layer of crème in between. Any variations of the Oreo (double stuff, fudge covered), would still encompass the main cookie concept. With one simple cookie idea, Nabisco successfully created an entire brand identity.

Now, say you want to pick up some cookies to impress your boss and your choices are a name brand, like Oreo, or an off-brand, such as Walmart's Great Value. Which will you choose? Probably the name brand. It shows that you spent a little more money and you know that the product will be good. Plus, it looks better. What if, instead of picking up cookies for your boss you are actually in charge of hiring an assistant for him/her. Are you going to choose the candidate with the stronger brand recognition, or the one that blends in with everyone else? I think the choice here is clear.

Think of yourself as a brand of cookies. What makes you different from all the other cookies? What makes you unique? Why would anyone purchase you over someone else? We'll go more in depth to your own personal brand in a minute, but first we should ask ourselves a very important question- why does it matter?

One of the most common misconceptions about personal branding is that it is egocentric and boastful. Knowing what makes you different and understanding the unique value you bring to a situation/organization/company is neither negative nor prideful; it's essential. There's a big difference between *knowing* your value and *gloating* your value to others. If you don't know your value, you won't be able to effectively sell yourself to others.

Think back to the muse or crush I asked you to come up with in the introduction. Do you know how she became the icon she is today? It may seem like good luck or simply being in the right place at the right time, but I guarantee it was much more than that. These individuals became household names because they intentionally decided to be seen a certain way. They cultivated a personal brand and used it to achieve their goals.

WHY YOU SHOULD CARE

I'm a big 'end goal' sort of person. Probably to an annoying extent. For every time I actually ask someone out loud, "what's your end goal here?" I have most likely asked that same question, a million times already in my head. It is especially prominent when someone, or a group of people in the case of corporations, makes what I would classify as a questionable decision. Have you ever seen a commercial that left you wondering who they were marketing to and what they were selling? Or maybe you see someone wearing full on pajamas in public and you can't help but think...'what???' Maybe it's just me, but I don't see the point of doing anything unless the ultimate end goal is worth achieving.

The great thing about personal branding is that when you figure out what your end goal is, you have the power to entirely change your life for the better. By answering that not so simple question, you are creating a framework for the rest of your life. Whether we consciously know it or not, our end goals dictate every action and decision we make on a day to day basis.

Confused? Let's go back to the cookie example. When Nabisco first decided to create the Oreo cookie, they started with a vision, and of course, an end goal. Now, I don't work on the Oreo marketing team and I definitely don't work for Nabisco, so I can't accurately tell you what Oreo's end goal is. However, we can make a few assumptions. Let's assume that Nabisco decided that it wanted to make an instantly recognizable, chocolate and crème cookie that would be paired perfectly with milk. It would be the first choice in chocolate cookies and would be always be associated with milk. Once the Oreo development team had that end goal in mind, getting there was probably relatively straightforward. I'm not going to say it was easy, because no product development is easy, but it was probably much easier than not having a clear definition of what exactly they were trying to develop.

Businesses do this all the time, although, they use the term 'mission statement' instead of end goal. A business, corporation, or an internal team usually always has a mission statement of something that they are trying to uphold or achieve. A mission statement is especially important as your business grows, to ensure that all employees are working towards the same goal. Just think, if the product development team at Nabisco is working to create the world's best chocolate cookie to be paired with milk while their marketing team is focused on promoting the brand as a health food pioneer, the brand will surely fail. It's only when there is a clear, effective mission statement that everyone is on board with, that will help lead a company to success. Can it guarantee success? Of course not. A great concept on paper isn't always viable when executed. A company needs to provide value to the consumer while also furthering its own agenda, all within the realms of what it is capable of doing best.

Take the outdoor clothing company Patagonia for example. It's not hard to find Patagonia's mission statement on their website. When you first log on to **www.patagonia.com** you will see only two menu options: shop and inside Patagonia. One helps the company's cash flow, while the other helps position the brand within the market. The first option under 'Inside Patagonia' is Our Mission Statement. Right there, first and foremost, Patagonia is saying, "hey, we want you to know who we are." Compared to other brands, their mission statement is relatively short. In fact, they don't even bother to throw a predicate in the sentence.

Patagonia's Mission Statement:
Build the best product, cause no unnecessary harm, use business to inspire and implement solutions to the environmental crisis.

In this one sentence statement, they are declaring their two biggest beliefs: good quality clothing and responsibility in the supply chain. The first belief is what fuels their economic engine while the second is what makes unwaveringly loyal customers. No matter what new initiatives or new products Patagonia team members are working on, they know they are moving in the right direction when their project will ultimately fulfil the end goal.

Big companies have mission statements, so what? What does that have to do with personal branding? And, more importantly, what does that have to do with you?

Here's the thing. If a business of any size can use a mission statement to be successful, then so can a person. But, just like a business needs to know what its brand is all about to create an effective mission statement, individuals also need to understand their own personal brands before they prescribe to life manifestos. If you have no idea who you are, what your strengths are, or what you're passionate about, writing, let alone living out, a mission statement is going to be incredibly difficult. Therefore, it only makes sense that we make an effort to discover our personal brand so that we can, in turn, create a strong mission statement for our lives.

Let's pause for a minute and ask my infamous question: to what end? What is the end goal of having an end goal? Hang on with me here, it's really not as nuanced as it seems. I'm simply asking, "What's the point of creating a mission statement for our lives?" Why even have an end goal? Why not just wander your way through life wherever the path takes you? I think the answer to those questions varies slightly from person to person, but it ultimately boils down to two things: 1) we want to feel like we have a purpose, and 2) we want to be successful.

Let's start with that first one. We all want to have a purpose. Every human has an innate need to be loved and accepted. We all want to feel like we matter. When we feel we have a purpose, we live better lives in the sense that we ourselves are happier and we also strive to make other people happier. It's that sense of purpose that helps us get up in the morning and keeps us from making bad decisions. With a purpose, we feel that others need us (that need to be accepted part) and that we matter (the need to be loved aspect).

The second part of this is a little trickier. We all want to be successful. I'm sure there are some people reading this who will say, 'well, I don't need money to make me happy. I don't need to be successful to have a good life.' While the fact that you don't need money to make you happy may be true, the part about not needing success is false. Maybe you don't need success in the sense that success is accumulated wealth. However, if you grew up in Western society, I am willing to bet that you feel the need to be successful, regardless of how you define success. Just as our culture has ingrained in us that helpful is a good thing, we have also learned that successful is a good thing. The key is to find the right definition for success that resonates with you. Quite literally, the definition of success is, "the accomplishment of an aim or purpose". Pretty vague right? If your aim is to learn something new every day, even failure in the traditional sense of the word can ultimately be success. The beauty of the term success is that you can really define it any way that works for you. Regardless of what your definition of success is, most of us are conditioned to need that feeling of accomplishment.

We all need to have a purpose. We all need to be successful. By having an end goal, personal mission statement, life manifesto- whatever you want to call it- we are fulfilling those needs. Just like those large companies, our personal mission statement gives us a path to follow and a purpose to live out. Unless you particularly enjoy bouncing through life without any sort of direction or intention, knowing your end goal, is the biggest secret to living a happy, successful, and thriving life.

THE SECRETS TO DISCOVERING YOUR PERSONAL BRAND

We can theorize about personal branding and mission statements all day, but unless we put any of it to practice in an applicable way, it doesn't do any good. Unless you understand what your personal brand is, the rest of this book will just be entertaining fluff. Here's the thing. I didn't sit down and write a book about how to make you look pretty. Yes, I am all about you looking fabulous, but my intent is to help you create a look and then use it to be successful. There are plenty of books out there on how to get dressed. There are even more on how to do it with style. I want to tell you how to alter your appearance to get what you want. Whether it's a better job, happier home life, or improved self-esteem, I want you to be living to your fullest potential. And that's something that needs to start from the inside, from your personal branding, and then move its way outward.

So, let's talk about your brand. I promise it will be easier than you think. Remember, we are trying to figure out what makes you, uniquely you. This includes personality traits, general characteristics, and accomplishments. It's everything that sets you apart from others in your home, office, town, state, and even country. Everyone has a personal brand, but most people's brands aren't realized or well developed. Using the following secrets, you can create a strong personal brand that will serve as a solid foundation for your future success!

Secret #1: Strong personal brands are a mix of intrinsic and extrinsic traits.

This is something a lot of people either forget, or disregard. Your personal brand isn't just about who you are, but what you've done, and how you've accomplished it. It's not just what you've done (e.g. Where you've gone to school, awards you've won, accounts you've landed...). It's not just about your personality (e.g. Extrovert, leader, intuitive...) or about how you your personality manifests itself (E.g. Outgoing, team player, problem solver...). Rather, a strong personal brand includes traits from all of these areas. There are several reasons why this is.

For one, it shows that there are multiple facets to you other than how you were born or what you've accomplished. Think about it. Any of the above characteristic sets can be entirely independent of another when creating a personal brand. One whole set of traits without any of the other sets leads the recipient to believe that you have certain qualities, but don't know how to use them. For example, if I say I am a Harvard graduate with a PhD in Biology and a successful career in research- that only describes my accomplishments. Alternatively, if that same person said, "I am an extrovert with a positive attitude and upbeat personality", they're really only talking about their intrinsic traits. The best personal brands show a blend of intrinsic and extrinsic traits. They declare, 'this is who I am and what I've achieved with what I've been given!' For example, it would be best if the above person said, 'I am an extroverted, ivy league graduate who is passionate about finding cures to common diseases in order to help everyday people." See how much more powerful it is when you combine the qualities you are born with and what you've accomplished?

Secret #2: Your personal brand is like a lock.

Remember those good old combination locks you were assigned in gym class during middle and high school? Every lock contained the same numbers, but each lock had their own special combination of those numbers that caused it to open up. Personal brands are very similar. The human population as a whole contains all the same characteristics, traits, and accomplishments. However, it's the way in which these are combined that make your personal brand special to you and unlock your full potential! Many people believe that they have to reinvent the wheel or discover a whole new personality trait in order to have a successful brand. This isn't true at all. The key isn't to make up characteristics that nobody else has, but rather to find the right combination of traits that you possess to create a new (or at least new to your desired audience) sequence. If you want to add some novelty into your combination, you do that by altering what you do or accomplish. For example, there are lots of philanthropic, anthropology graduates. However, there are much fewer philanthropic, anthropology graduates that have devoted significant amounts of time to studying a specific species of animal just as Jane Goodall studied apes.

There is no one size fits all method to identifying your personal brand. However, I usually recommend that people narrow down their five strongest descriptors and use that as their personal brand. Just as a combination lock may be 12 + 4 + 7 + 22 + 35 = open, your personal brand can do the same with this simple formula: intrinsic personality trait + accomplishment + general characteristic + goal + passion = winning personal brand! In a sentence it would look like, 'My name is Kathy and I am an extroverted, award winning research scientist who uses my compassionate nature to pursue the cure for cancer and help everyone I come in contact with.' Each of the individual parts of this sentence are true for hundreds of people, but when you pull together the parts that are uniquely yours, then you can accurately describe your own personal brand.

Just think of your personal brand statement as a 'cut to the chase' elevator speech. In a few seconds or less, what do you want the other person to know about you? With a successful elevator speech or personal brand statement you lay down your most important cards, and in doing so, will attract others who share the same passions and goals as you. Here's a personal example of how a strong personal brand statement can help you. A few months ago, I was attending a small entrepreneurial networking session and we had the opportunity to introduce ourselves. Some of the attendees seemed caught off guard and stuttered a short line of thoughts like, "well, I'm Jake and my wife and I are thinking about possibly starting a fishing business, maybe". Other people, like myself, confidently threw out their personal brand statements along with an invitation to talk afterwards. I think I used some version of, "Hi, My name is Leslie Friedman. I'm an author, speaker and image consultant who is passionate about helping people leverage their personal brands and their appearances to be more successful. I really enjoy collaborating with other entrepreneurs, so don't be shy to come say hi after the program; I'd love to talk to you." It is simple and to the point. Not every person in the room found me after the program to say hi, but the ones that did were also aligned with my goals and came with opportunities. A solid personal brand statement not only helps you keep focused, but it is a key component to opening doors.

Secret #3: Don't forget about your end goal.

I'm sure you have a lot of characteristics, goals, passions, accomplishments, and traits that define you. The key to picking the right ones for a strong personal brand depend on what you want to accomplish with your brand. Remember when we talked about your end goal and having a mission statement? If you don't know what your end goal is, then it will be very difficult to pull together a personal brand that will lead you there. Just as you need to pick the right paint when painting different parts of a house, you need to find the right combination of attributes that will help you accomplish your end goal best. If the aforementioned, bio-scientist Kathy wants to help elementary aged children by having a long career as a second grade teacher, then her personal branding statement is way off. If her goal is to be a notable, bio-researcher with a significant influence in the realm of disease prevention, then she is right on track. Nabisco probably had a clear end goal in mind when they created Oreo, and they made sure that the branding around the Oreo cookie ensured the success of reaching that goal. In this same way, we need to make sure our brand is properly setting us up for our end goals.

Secret #4: The easiest way to discover your brand is by not trying.

Your personal brand is 100% you and there's no one who has a clearer view of you than those around you. So, if you're stumped about what your brand is, sit back and let the people around you throw in their input. Simply ask any objective, third party person who spends time around you (a coworker is a great option) to describe who you are. Better yet, have them describe you to another coworker. The more people you sample, the better picture you will be able to make about yourself. It is also worthwhile to ask the people that know you the best (spouses, family members, friends) how they would describe you. Most likely, your personal brand is going to be a combination of the two opinions. While this is one of the most effective ways to find out what your personal brand is, it can also be the most painful- especially if you're not branding yourself to your fullest potential.

If other's responses are way off base compared to how you would describe yourself, your brand is having an identity crisis. Look into inconsistencies and ask yourself 1) which way you would like to be seen and 2) what you're doing to elicit an undesired response. Maybe you think working through your lunch hour every day brands you as hardworking and dedicated, but really it comes off as aloof and as a bad team player.

Even if you have your personal brand down pat (these are the traits I want to be known for!) it's important to consistently ask for feedback to make sure your branding is accurate. Large companies are constantly soliciting feedback on their products and their brand image to ensure that the image they are presenting to the consumer is exactly the branding they desire. Find the combination of attributes that is most accurate for you and most effective to reaching your end goal and then double check it over year after year to make sure you are always on track for success.

Secret #5: Your personal brand might change. And that's okay.

The personal brand you develop during the length of this book may not be the same brand you have in twenty years. It may not even be the brand you have in five or ten years, and to be completely honest, it shouldn't be. Hopefully, you are constantly in the process of developing and growing into a bigger and better person. Throughout your life you will have different accomplishments, experiences, and encounters that affect your goals, missions, and values. You will also have different priorities today than ten years from now. If you're a young, professional making their mark in the workplace, you may place more value on being seen as knowledgeable and experienced. Ten or fifteen years down the road, however, you may place more value on being known as a leader and a great communicator. The key is to constantly reassess your mission statement and your personal brand statement to ensure that it aligns up with who you want to be today and the short term future. When you are younger, your brand statement may change as much as every year to every five years, while at the peak of your career, it will probably change every ten to fifteen years.

Coming up with a personal brand that is reflective of your true self shouldn't be difficult. If you're forcing a certain goal or character trait on yourself that doesn't come naturally or that you aren't passionate about, you'll have a hard time living out your brand. It's much easier and less energy consuming to actively develop and pursue a brand that feels like second nature. To get started discovering your ideal personal brand (at least for right now!) use the worksheet at the end of this chapter.

PERSONAL BRANDING EXERCISE

This easy activity will help you start formulating your personal brand.

List 5 intrinsic personality traits that describe you

_____

_____

_____

_____

_____

List 5 accomplishments that you've achieved

_____

_____

_____

_____

_____

List 5 other general characteristics about yourself

_____

_____

_____

_____

_____

List 5 goals you wish to accomplish

_____

_____

_____

_____

List 5 things you are passionate about

_____

_____

_____

_____

_____

Now, go back to your goals list and number them in importance from 1-5 (1 being a goal that you would be okay not accomplishing and 5 being a goal that you would want written in an obituary). Your #5 goal, and potentially #4 goal are going to shape your mission statement. They are also going to decide what other traits your personal brand should highlight. With these goals in mind, go back through the other four lists and rank the items in every list from 1-5 with 1 being most likely trait to help with your specified goals and 5 being least likely. For example, if Kathy the bio scientist who wants to help others (goal) and cure the world of cancer (another goal) is ranking her general characteristics, she would give 'compassionate' a higher score than 'funny' because it is more in line with aforementioned goals.

Once you have the top pick from each list, string them together in a coherent manner. This sequence is a good starting point:
Intrinsic personality trait + accomplishment + general characteristic + goal + passion = personal brand statement

Using the above formula, Kathy's personal brand statement sounded like this: My name is Kathy and I am an extroverted, award winning research scientist who uses my compassionate nature to pursue the cure for cancer and help everyone I come in contact with.

Her mission statement may sound something like this: My goal is to help find a cure for cancer through medical research.

Obviously, that's quite a lofty goal. Your goal (and subsequently your personal brand statement) needs to resonate with your life. If you are a teacher your goal may be to help students make wise decisions or become independent adults. A manager may wish to be a positive role model for his employees and his family. It doesn't need to be elaborate, but it does need to exist. If you don't know what you're working towards, you'll never intentionally get there.

Chapter 2:

It's all in the packaging.

Long before I started Image Consulting and Public Speaking, I worked in fashion, designing women's apparel. While designing several private labels of women's clothing and working closely with customers, I realized that the majority of people have no idea how to dress themselves. To clarify, they knew how to put clothes on their body, but unless outfits were styled for them on a mannequin they couldn't put together a good outfit to save their lives. That's when I slowly moved over to the image consulting world. I would help clients clean out their closets, sort through clothes, go shopping, and dress for specific events like weddings, interviews, and new jobs. Today, I primarily work with executives while managing my online image consulting service (www.leslie-friedman.com).

Every time I consult a client about their wardrobe, whether online or in person, the conversation starts with enquiries into their personal brand. What they want it to be. What it actually is. The conversation usually consists of phrases like, "how do you want others to see you?" And "do you have any icons whose lives, style, etc. you admire?" Rather than, "so, let's talk about your personal brand..." But those former questions lead me exactly to what I need to know to assess their wardrobe (and ultimately, fix whatever issue I've been called in for). Personal branding starts each client session for the same reason that it starts this book: it's the foundation you need in order to leverage your appearance successfully.

Of course, you can have a great appearance without a solid foundation of branding, but if you want to be able to use it to be more successful, happy, or satisfied, then you are going to need something deeper than just a flippant desire to 'dress better' (whatever that means). This is why people roll their eyes and dismiss the overused cliché 'dress for success'. Success means different things to different people and until you figure out who you are and where you want to go, then it will mean nothing.

It's ironic to me the quantity of personal branding gurus out there that have a complete lack of presence, power over their appearance, and/or understanding of the importance of great design. That last point, great design, is something we won't talk about in this book, but I'm referring to website, logo, business card design, etc. It's ironic because the very thing they are overlooking is one of the most important parts of their brand: the packaging.

Let's talk about cookies again. Imagine you created a cookie that is leaps and bounds better than any other cookie on the planet. You're a nice person (not to mention the fact that you think you can start an epic cookie empire with your to-die-for recipe) so you decide to package and market your cookies so that the world can enjoy your magical creation. In an effort to save money with your cookie start-up, you choose to use basic packaging consisting of a brown paper bag that is sealed at the top and contains the words, '[your name]'s Fantastic Cookies'. Pictures would take up too much ink, so you just include some more words: 'chocolatey, chewy pieces of heaven in your mouth'. You don't really feel the need to write too much because they are the best cookies in the world. Now it's time to sell your product. You take it to a big food fair and to a local market to pitch your cookies to both grocery retailers and customers. At the end of the day you are disappointed to realize that your cookies did not garner much interest. Grocery chains didn't give you the time of day and customers didn't give you a second glance. Your multimillion cookie empire is crumbling before it even starts, leaving you to wonder: what went wrong?

You don't have to be a marketing wizard to figure out why your cookie business didn't work out. It's pretty obvious that your packaging was not serving your product justice. Bad packaging can ruin even the best product. There's a reason nobody pulls a diamond ring out a greasy plastic bag to propose to their loved one. Packaging tells the viewer what kind of quality they can expect from the product. An engagement ring in a chintzy plastic ring box is going to be viewed as far inferior than one in a velvet covered, silk lined ring box.

Likewise, your appearance sets the stage for your personal brand. It not only tells people what kind of quality to expect from you, but it conveys what your brand is before you even get a chance to speak. Remember your poorly packaged cookies? The only chance you have of selling them is to probably sample them out. Once you gave someone a sample, then they would realize they were the best cookies in the world and would be more willing to buy your product. Unfortunately for us, we don't always get the chance to sample ourselves out. Like all the grocers and potential customers that walked by your booth, future clients and employees come in and out of your daily life constantly (and usually without your knowledge). You don't always get to tell these people how talented, sociable, and hardworking you are. All they have to create an opinion of you is how you look. This is why your appearance is important, and this is why I truly believe that by changing your appearance you can change your entire life.

The first thing that comes to mind for most people when I mention the words 'image' and 'appearance' is clothing and accessories. While your clothes do make up a part of your appearance, they by no mean constitute the whole. Your whole image is what sociologists call your 'dress'. Your dress is anything that makes up your appearance, from (yes) your clothes, to your body language, to your tattoos and piercings.

LET'S START WITH THE CLOTHES

I like to start with the clothes because, as I mentioned before, they are the foremost thought when people think of image. Since clothes (hopefully) cover up a significant part of your body, they are often the quickest ways to communicate your brand. In fact, clothes are so good at communicating status, position, and rank that we cognitively make them specific parts of many careers. We can easily identify military officials, medical workers, and McDonald's employees all by the uniforms that they wear. Kings and Queens can wear crowns and opulent clothing because they don't need to move quickly or physically work, while lifeguards on a beach need to don hats for sun protection and certain swimwear that is specifically designed to make them identifiable and to help them perform their duty effectively. Even if you don't wear a formal uniform everyday like a physician, fast food worker, or flight attendant would, your clothing choice is still sending a message to the world.

Subconsciously, you are probably aware of what messages certain articles of clothing and entire outfits send. Suits generally make you look more professional, while sweatpants make you look careless, or at best, athletic. It's easy to tell someone that if they wish to be seen as more professional, that they should wear a suit. However well intentioned, this isn't always good advice. If you borrow a suit that is too big for you, you're going to come off as sloppier than if you had just stayed in your khakis and polo that fit. If you're a bar owner meeting with customers, a suit may come off as way too fussy. Depending on your situation and what you want to accomplish, different clothing can send different messages. This is one of the fundamental flaws in the one size fits all advice about 'dressing for success'.

So how do we choose clothes that reflect our brand? How do we know what hard working looks like when we look in a mirror? Or dedicated? Or genuine? It's certainly not easy, and there's no right or wrong answers. In fact, the way we answer those questions depends on everything from your age and sex to what part of the country you live in and what you do for a living. With that said, I am able to provide some general guidelines on what to wear depending on how you'd like to be branded. Below, I will go through some of the most popular characteristics people would like to be known for, and how that translates into your clothing. This is the time to look back at the personal brand statement you created in chapter 1 and see if any of the intrinsic qualities or general characteristics from your brand are listed below.

Articulate (also: detail oriented) *Adj. 1. Able to express ideas clearly and effectively in speech or writing*
Articulate people pay attention to details and they put a good amount of thought into their words and actions. You can easily carry these same traits over to your dress, by paying attention to the details of your appearance and thoughtfully choosing your ensembles. Make an effort to keep all parts of your appearance 'under control' by avoiding things such as unkempt hair and free flowing clothing. Precise, classically tailored clothing will send the message of articulate any day over a loose t-shirt and baggy jeans.

Authentic (also: genuine) *Adj. 1. Real or genuine: not copied or false. 2. True and accurate*
The easiest way to start looking authentic, is to stop looking fake-something that is often easier said than done. Depending on how long we've been faking things about our appearance we may become

numb to the inauthenticity of our image. For example, someone who tans excessively may be so used to seeing themselves a dark shade of brown that they may not realize that it looks unnatural. Likewise, someone who uses excessive amounts of makeup may not realize that they have the appearance of looking fabricated. Does that mean you need to go au naturel in order to be seen as authentic? No, of course not. But what you do need to do is find a balance that is representative of who you are and how you want to be seen. You can use clothing, makeup, changes in hair, skin color, piercings, etc. to enhance your natural self, however, it should support and not distract from your brand.

Competent. *Adj. 1. Having suitable or sufficient skill, knowledge, experience, etc., for some purpose; properly qualified*
There's a scene from the 1990's classic movie "Joe versus the Volcano" where Joe walks into his horrible office and you can hear a fellow employee repeatedly yelling into his phone, "I know he can get the job, but can he do the job?" None of us want to seem like we can't do the job and we definitely don't want to hire people that can't do the job. We work hard in high school, college, and internships to gain the skills necessary to be competent in various industries. Unfortunately, our appearance has the ability to undermine our skills and leave us looking sadly incompetent. To combat this, start by looking appropriate for your profession and then dress the age you wish your competency level to be perceived. If I'm a 25 year old law school graduate clerking with a local judge, I'm going to dress professionally and probably a bit older than my age. If I'm an experienced, 40 year old fashion designer in New York City, I will dress in a creative, yet classy way that is appropriate for my current age. If you dress different than what is expected in your industry or profession, you will look, at best, like you are above everyone else, or at worst, like you have no clue what's going on. The last thing you want is for someone to look at you and say, "That can't be the right person. He looks like he would know nothing about xyz…" You'll want

to adjust the age appropriateness of your dress based on whether you want to seem more experienced or credible. A younger, less experienced professional may choose to dress a bit older to garner more respect. Meanwhile, an established professional is better off dressing within 5-7 years of their actual age.

Creative. *Adj. 1. Having or showing an ability to make new things or think of new ideas*
It's important to realize, that you don't have to look like Billy Idol, Lady Gaga, or like you just walked out of a Commes Des Garcons store to appear creative. Sometimes all it takes is doing something just a bit more innovative with your wardrobe than everyone else in your immediate vicinity. This may mean mixing a print and a pattern, donning a bold pattern, or belting a jacket instead of buttoning it. The key is to show that you understand the norm and that you are willing to think out of the box. If your outfit is a bit out of the box (once again, this doesn't have to be radical- wearing a printed blouse under your suit in your corporate office may be enough) and it looks good, then people will think of you has a successful risk taker, problem solver, and creative out of the box thinker.

Dependable *(see also: reliable, trustworthy)*. *Adj. Able to be trusted to do or provide what is needed: able to be depended on*
If you look like you can't take care of yourself, then people will assume you can't take care of anything else. That seems harsh, but it's true. Imagine you are hiring a dog walker to come exercise your new puppy while you're at work. You have the choice between two employees. Dog Walker #1 is neatly groomed while Dog Walker #2 looks dishevelled and barely pulled together. Who are you going to hire? Chances are you are going to choose Walker #1 because they at least look like they can take care of themselves (let alone your pricey new golden doodle). When you look like you can take care of yourself and trust yourself, it gives other people permission to do the same.

Funny. *Adj. 1. Causing laughter*

This is a common adjective that many people use to describe themselves and their brand, but it's one of the harder ones to translate into clothing. Unless your occupation is a clown, or some other circus entity, then give up on trying to look funny. Instead, the adjectives you'll want to channel when it comes to dressing are more along the lines of humorous, quirky, and fun. Wearing Darth Vader dress socks shows you have a sense of humor. Dressing as Darth Vader shows that you forgot you're at work and not Comicon. Mixing and matching prints and patterns shows you have a fun quirky side. Wearing graphic tees or shirts with funny sayings makes you look, at worst, painfully unprofessional at and, at best, like you robbed your kid's closet.

Generous. *Adj. 1. Providing more than the amount that is needed or normal: abundant or ample*

There's only so many hours in a day, therefore, the more time you spend on others, the less time you'll have for yourself. Am I suggesting you walk around constantly dishevelled because you don't have time to take care of yourself? Of course not. In fact, you need to take care of yourself so that you have the energy to give back to others. The key is to strike the perfect balance between a high maintenance and low maintenance look. Imagine that you walk into a soup kitchen and see two women serving the soup. One has highlighted hair, perfectly polished acrylic nails, and diamond studs while the other has natural colored hair pulled back in a ponytail with unpolished nails and no jewelry. If both women are wearing the same jeans and t-shirt, you'll almost always view the latter as more generous than the former for two reasons: 1- she looks like she has less to give and therefore her generosity carries more weight and 2- your first thought when you see her is 'she is here helping out because she cares about these people' where you might think 'she's a well put together lady with money' when you see the other woman. There's nothing wrong with looking put together or appearing to have money, but if you want to seem generous, the first impression people make of you needs to be about others rather than yourself.

Happy. *Adj. 1. Delighted, pleased, or glad, as over a particular thing*
The easiest way to dress happier is to wear more prints and colors. While, I love the color black, there's nothing happy about somber colors that were once reserved purely for funeral wear. Instead, think of the fun colors used in resort wear clothing. Resort wear is exactly what it sounds like: clothing intended to be worn on vacation, specifically at a resort. Because of the nature of resort clothing, it is almost always produced in bright, fun colors and bold patterns to reflect the happiness we feel when on vacation.

Independent. *Adj. 1. Not subject to control by others. 2. Not requiring or relying on something else*
Independent is a common character trait that many young professionals, specifically college graduates, want to be known as. They are eager to break away from the ties that bind (that's you, parents) and try to make their way in the world. If you are one such person, the best way for you to look independent is to do things you may not have being doing previously- like ironing your shirts. Or ironing anything for that matter. I knew a young woman in management who needed to wear an ironed shirt because of an upcoming corporate visit. She went out and purchased an iron, ironed the shirt, and then returned the iron as if she was never going to need it again. Her first two decisions were great. The last one, not so much. If you want to be seen as an independent adult, you are going to have to do some adult things like ironing, purchasing professional clothing, getting your clothes tailored, finding and using a dry cleaners, etc. It sounds obvious, but it needs to be said nonetheless. Is there anything you don't do because someone else has always done it for you and now that they are gone, you simply choose to 'go without'? Although

not always, these are often the very things that help us look independent.

Intelligent (also: intellectual, emotionally intelligent). *Adj. 1. Having or showing the ability to easily learn or understand things or to deal with new or difficult situations: having or showing a lot of intelligence*
While a good pair of glasses and a tweed jacket can be effective in making you seem intelligent (yes, it's weird but it's true), there are other ways to display this trait. One of the best ways to show your intelligence is to put it to work by being resourceful and doing your research. If you're going somewhere, figure out what clothing is appropriate for your destination. This may sound really obvious, but failing to bring a coat on a long weekend to Boston in the winter doesn't exactly make you seem like the brightest bulb in the closet. Likewise, showing up to a black tie wedding in cocktail attire makes you look incapable of even googling basic dress codes. Actually take a moment to think through your clothing choices, and if you're at a loss, then put your brain (or computer) to work finding an answer.

Kind. (also closely related to loving) *Adj. 1. Of a good or benevolent nature or disposition, as a person*
While it isn't always the case, kindness is often associated with softness. The kind of softness I'm referring to isn't the same as weakness, rather, it's more the opposite of harsh. When your appearance reflects kindness, it also gravitates more toward soft looks than harsh ones. Soft looks include lighter colors, physically softer fabrics, and more feminine details like ruffles and flounces. Harsh looks include darker colors like black, and have more geometric silhouettes without unnecessary details. Soft and harsh looks both have their time and place, but if you want people to see kindness when they see you, opt for softer ensembles.

Loving. (also: caring, compassionate) *Adj. 1. Feeling or showing love. 2. Very careful and thorough*

The way to look loving is very similar to the way to look dependable. It starts with making sure that you look like you are applying the desired attribute to yourself. If you don't look like you love yourself, then it's going to be hard to imagine you loving someone else. Take care of your body, your skin, your hair, your clothing, etc. and you will look like you respect and love yourself. With that said, don't go overboard on the self-love. People who appear to have spent way too much time on themselves will be thought of as egocentric and selfish rather than loving.

Passionate. *Adj. 1. Having, showing, or expressing strong emotions or beliefs*

Here's some good news: you don't have to resort to a graphic tee to show the world you're passionate about something (unless you love tee-shirts, in which case, I'm sorry). One of the best ways to show you are passionate through your clothing is to adapt garments that allow you to live out your passion easily and to the best of your ability. If you're a lawyer who is passionate about human rights advocacy, then you will dress in a way that will reflect positively upon you and your clients in a courtroom. If you are passionate about teaching, then you will dress in a way that shows your students you're serious about the subject matter and about them. For a business teacher, this may mean dressing in a business casual or business professional manner to be an example to the kids. Or, if you're a middle school math teacher, it could mean wearing jeans to better relate to your students. It all comes down to dressing in a way that respects the work you are doing and the other people that are involved.

Professional. *Adj. 1. Relating to a job that requires special education, training, or skill*

This is an adjective that most young people, especially those just embarking on new careers, what to be known for. While the exact clothing items that go into play with professional dress vary from industry to job type, there are few common ties among all professional looking clothing. It is clean and devoid of stains, holes, and general dirtiness and destruction. Professional clothing fits. It fits the wearer exactly the way it was designed to fit. This means no bulges, stretch lines, sagging parts, or uneven hems. Lastly, all professional clothing is appropriate. It is appropriate for the wearer's age, sex, body shape, job title, etc.

Relatable. Adj. 1. *Being able to establish a social or sympathetic relationship with a person or thing*
Looking relatable is as easy as a quick study into the market you're trying to relate to. The hardest part, is probably taking the time to figure out who we actually want to relate to us. Is our main priority our clients, teachers, employers, or our kids? It will be very difficult, if not impossible, to relate to multiple different groups at the same time. We need to pick who the most important target market is at any given time. Your Tuesday afternoon meeting with a potential vendor may cause you to dress a completely different way than your Wednesday morning meeting with your child's teacher. You need to figure out who your audience is, and then dress in a similar manner to them. For example, if your boss usually wears a suit and tie, then you should also wear a suit and tie during important business meetings with him. If the other parents at your child's baseball games usually wear jeans and casual tops, then you might also want to wear casual clothing. You don't need to copy someone's look head to toe (that's creepy), but you do want to send the message, 'hey look, I am one of you! I belong'.

HAIR, MAKEUP, EYEWEAR, AND ACCESSORIES

Unfortunately, when it comes to your image, clothing gets way too much attention while everything else falls to the wayside. Have you ever seen someone and just had 'a weird feeling' about them that you just can't figure out? They might be well dressed, but somehow something is sending off subliminal yellow flags in your mind and you can't really put your finger on it. This is probably because your whole appearance is vital in communicating. When one part (let's say clothing) sends one message and another aspect (like body language) sends a contradictory message, the viewer's subconscious picks up on the conflict of messages and throws up that yellow (or sometimes red) flag. There's a reason why we are told to 'go with your gut'. That gut feeling is really just the result of your mind picking up on nonverbal communication and compiling it all together in a handy, easy to read 'this is good', 'watch out, or 'you're in danger' message.

These 'quick reads' your gut gives you were all once a grand scheme to keep you alive during the Palaeolithic era. Fortunately for us, what once worked for cavemen still works today. That's because our mind scans for inconsistencies in general, rather than specific points. For example, if another cave man walked up to your clan wearing a familiar outfit, and claimed to be friend, yet displayed aggressive body language you would probably be on your guard. You aren't really analyzing why you feel cautious around this other person, but you know things aren't adding up. The inconsistencies tell you that this foreign caveman may be untrustworthy, and that is far more important than the small details. On the other hand, if a cave man walks up to your clan wearing a foreign animal skin and asks for directions because he was lost, all while displaying peaceful body language, you would be much more apt to trust this person and help him out. The point is, the more consistent with your personal brand your entire image is, the stronger the sense of trustworthiness is that you send. The more trustworthy you are (or at least appear) the more people will be willing to work with you, hire you, and help you achieve your goals.

The key to forming a consistent personal brand is to make sure that every part of your image tells the message you want to send. Little things like hairstyles, makeup, and eyewear are extremely important because each of these are either surrounding or directly on your face: the place others see first when they look at us. Other accessories, like shoes, handbags, briefcases, etc. are also important as they are often send mixed messages about our brand. We'll start with the top of the body and work our way down.

Hair

When it comes to hair, most people fall into one of two groups: they either don't like their hair or they don't care. For whatever reason, the majority of people (yes, even those with to die for locks) will find a reason to complain. Too thick, too thin, too straight, too curly. I would argue, however, that 99.9% of these complaints are unfounded as everyone has something lovely about their hair. At any rate, you don't have to love your hair, but you do have to love the message it sends. Ignoring your hair because you don't like it, sticking to the same haircut for decades because 'it's the only one that looks good on you', and/or simply not caring are all bad for your personal brand.

If you could care less about your hair or simply pull it back in a ponytail because you don't want to deal with it, now's the time to stop. If you want to be seen as any of the following: articulate, professional, detail oriented, respectable, current, a good time manager, and/or trustworthy, then you need to start doing something to your hair. The good news is that you don't necessarily have to do a lot. Find a good hair stylist and be brutally honest with them. They are professionals; seek their help. I am lazy when it comes to hair care and I make sure my stylist knows it. As a result, she gives me easy to maintain cuts and advises me on simple styles that are quick and classy. Be sure to relay to your stylist what characteristics you are looking for in a cut and show pictures of people who embody those traits and share a similar hair type as you. For example: "I need a no fuss hairstyle that looks professional and sophisticated much like Melinda Gates in this picture (show picture)."

Maybe you've found a style that is really working for you and you're holding on tight for dear life. Congratulations! You've done the hardest part: identifying the perfect color and cut for your face. Now what you need to do is make sure that your hairstyle doesn't overstay its welcome. We've all know that one person that clings onto a hairstyle for decades. What was once a flattering, in-style hair cut is now tired and antiquated. If you want to be seen as modern, up to date, and relatable, you need to look like you are at least aware of what the current decade is. Try to change your hair up every 3-5 years to avoid looking out of touch. If the thought of changing up your beloved hairstyle throws you into a total panic, don't worry. You already know what shapes work best with your face, so you simply need to change up the length, layers, etc. to keep the look modern. Have you ever seen one of those 'through the decades' pictures that show headshots of prominent actors/actresses over the course of several decades? You'll notice that the hairstyles rarely deviate too much from their general shape (with the exception of the occasional unfortunate younger year photos) but they do change slightly to become more modern. Jennifer Aniston is a great example of this. Her hairstylist knows that layers framing her face look best. Throughout the years, her hairstyles change in length and texture, but they almost always include layers that frame the face. This is exactly what you want to achieve.

Remember, your hair is the frame for your face. If you put a beautiful Monet painting in a cheap frame, people will assume the painting is not legitimate. Keep your hair style consistent with the rest of your visual brand and you are well on your way to coming across more trustworthy, current, and approachable.

Eyewear

The same rules for hair also apply to eyewear for (surprise, surprise) exactly the same reasons. Eyewear goes through trends, just like anything else, and while you don't have to try every trend, you do need to modernize your eyeglasses every 3-5 years. In fact, you really shouldn't follow every trend. You'll end up spending a lot of money buying into fads that may not be flattering and will only make you seem like you're trying too hard. Instead, it's best to approach eyewear trends the same way as hair trends- find a good shape that works well for your face and then alter it in size, material, etc. every couple years. For example, if you know rectangular glasses look best on you, stick with that shape and experiment with smaller or larger frames, or try different colors. If you change up your eyewear too drastically (unless it is a specific part of your brand and something you'd like to be known for) or too often you will send the message of inconsistency, which as you'll remember, is directly correlated to untrustworthiness.

If you're not sure what shape of frames look best on your face, do some research and go to an eyeglass shop that knows what they're doing. Try on as many pairs as you can and don't neglect your gut instinct. If you look in the mirror and immediately think, 'ugh' then put them back. If you make a bad first impression on yourself, then it will be bad for everyone else also. With that said, don't be afraid to go a little out of your comfort zone.

When it comes to most small ticket items, I am a speed shopper. I know what I like and I know what works for me and, probably most importantly, I don't buy anything unless I instantly love the product. Whether it's a house or a new blouse I do my research, but don't linger on the decision process. Occasionally, however, I do break the mold and really have to take a moment. This happened a couple of years ago when I bought a new pair of glasses. Big glasses had just come into fashion and I was ready to trade out my smaller frames for ones with more substance. The first pair I picked out happened to be perfect. They fit my face great, they were just the color I wanted, and they were big without being too big. However, quite out of character, I didn't purchase them immediately. Something about the way they looked on me seemed funny. After trying on a million more pairs and staring at myself way too long in the mirror, I realized that the first ones were great. My original hesitation was simply because I wasn't used to seeing myself in bigger frames. I knew I liked the way I looked in them, but I was a little too stretched outside my comfort zone to take the leap. In the end, it was worth it. I've received lots of compliments on my frames and I actually make a point to wear them instead of contacts. Stick to what looks good on you, but don't be afraid to experiment a bit.

The right, modern frame for your face should enhance your eyes without completely taking over the show. Bold eyewear is a great choice, especially if you want to draw the attention away from other places. No one is going to be ogling your self-declared flaws if they are constantly drawn back to your face. In general, glasses make people seem more intelligent and knowledgeable, even if they aren't. I would often wear glasses in my early 20's when I wanted to come across as older, more sophisticated, and intellectual. Regardless of your age, remember to switch frames every 3-5 years to appear more up to date, attentive, and relatable.

Makeup

People are shallow creatures. This really shouldn't come as news to you. No matter how much we claim to be unbiased and concerned about 'what's on the inside', we can't help the fact that we still take in and process the information we are seeing on the outside. Studies show that prettier people (technically, those are people who have the highest amount of symmetry in their features) have better jobs, are more successful, and are simply treated better by others. Is it fair? Absolutely not! But, while we can't change our features without cosmetic surgery, we can change little aspects that make us seem more beautiful. Hence: makeup.

Everyone has a sweet spot when it comes to makeup. In my opinion, the perfect amount of makeup is just enough to enhance your positive traits while downplaying your less attractive features all while making it appear that you are, in fact, wearing no makeup. Seem hard? That's because it is. Anyone can avoid makeup altogether; that's easy. Likewise, most women are very capable of piling it all on and going a bit overboard. It really gets hard when you try to find that happy medium, which is why there are countless YouTube videos, Pinterest tutorials, and Facebook infographics showing you how to achieve the 'nude look'. It's really ironic, but for whatever reason, success comes to those who look like they were born this (very, naturally pretty) way.

Just like everything else we are discussing, makeup sends messages to others. A full face of heavy makeup subliminally says that you are trying to hide, or make up for some insecurities. On the other hand, no makeup (unless you are gifted with a spotless complexion) can make the individual seem careless, bad with time management, and/or like they don't respect themselves. Am I saying that if you show up with going out makeup to the next board meeting or with a naked face to the next interview that you are going to fail at life? No, but you certainly aren't helping yourself out any. Using makeup, even in minimal amounts, is simply using all the cards that are being dealt to you. Wearing makeup can also be a sign of respect for the other person. Even minimal makeup says, 'I realized you had to look at me today, so I made sure to look my best.' While many people consider wearing makeup to be vain, I think it's a considerate gesture. Remember, the amount of time you look at yourself in a day is drastically lower than the amount of time others will spend looking at you. So, take an extra moment to put on foundation and some mascara and you will look like you made the extra effort to do something for those around you (no matter how naturally beautiful you may be).

Accessories

Shoes, briefcases, purses, ties, socks, belts, hats, watches, and jewelry. These are just a few items that come into play when discussing accessories. They are the extras that can make or break an outfit, or equally so, someone's impression of you. As Forrest Gump so accurately claimed and later studies actually proved, "...you can tell a lot about a person by their shoes". I would argue that the same goes for most accessories.

Accessories are usually very personal belongings that really show insight into the person wearing them. We often invest more in our handbags, briefcases, shoes, and jewelry so the items tend to be closer in step with our personality because we truly love what we are willing to spend more money on. Therefore, the type of accessory and the condition it's in can tell you a lot about a person. A woman who always wears matching jewelry sets may be more comfortable in a structured setting, less creative, and/or possibly like to be in control. A man with a nicer suit, but inappropriate footwear and a cheap briefcase may be more apt to cutting corners, less detail oriented, and/or more concerned about function and efficiency. Of course, a person who is completely dishevelled can be a creative genius (remember what Einstein looked like?) but it's going to take a lot more effort otherwise for the general populace to take that person seriously.

Think about the last time you attended a birthday party where cake was involved. My guess is the cake wasn't completely naked; it probably had some sort of icing. I'm also willing to bet that there was something more than just your basic buttercream frosting. Maybe some icing flowers, sprinkles, written words, or even fruit. While I'm sure you would be excited about just a basic cake with ordinary frosting (I mean, who doesn't love cake?) your expectations of how delicious the cake is will probably rise with how well it's decorated. A deluxe seven layer cake with dozens of ornate icing blossoms will probably lead you to believe the cake has been prepared with care and therefore, will be delicious. You feel honored to be invited to an event with such a cake. The same concept can be applied to our appearance. You are this amazing, talented cake and the basic frosting is your clothing. You can make a statement with only your basic frosting, but it looks much more professional, and the whole wow factor comes together, when you start adding the finishing touches: sprinkles, icing flowers, etc. These, of course, are your accessories. If you are going to take all the effort to create a great cake (think: your school degrees, all that character development, and every self-help book you've read) then you should make sure that everyone else knows, just by looking at it, that it's a cake you don't want to pass up. So, choose accessories that will work well with your outfit and will improve your entire look. Remember that we are working towards making sure your entire appearance is consistent, and streamlining your accessories to your personal brand is a great way to do that.

If you're going to put your money anywhere, I recommend you splurge on high quality, classic accessories. A nice watch shows that you are conscientious about time and that you aren't fully dependant on your cell phone (looking at you millennials). A polished briefcase or purse shows that you respect your work documents and tote them around with care. Clean, polished, and professional shoes demand respect and elevate your status in the eyes of others. A coordinating (two different fabrics/prints that go well together) pocket square and tie show a creative person who pays attention to details while a matching (same fabric/print) tie and square show that you take yourself seriously and that you like structure and control. Tasteful jewelry that isn't overwhelming or overly extravagant tells a story and makes you seem more relatable and friendly. Hats are tricky, but can be used effectively to portray different messages. A CEO can be more relevant to his hourly workers if he dons a baseball cap and jeans to the company picnic. A woman or man can command immediate attention in a room with a more formal hat reminiscent of the 40's and 50's. Study the accessories of people you admire. How do they play into the way you perceive the person as a whole? How can you adapt some of these same accessory ideas to create the same image about yourself?

If you're not sure what your accessories are telling people, then ask! The more anonymity you give to the person responding, the more truthful your answer will be. Take a picture of any questionable accessories and show them to a coworker or someone that doesn't realize the item is yours. Ask them what they think in general and if they think a [insert how you want to be branded] person would wear the item. If they think you're asking a general question, they should respond quite truthfully. If it's a big purchase that you're thinking about, and not something you already own, you may want to get several opinions.

HOW YOU MOVE YOUR BODY COUNTS TOO

If it weren't trouble enough to put on the right clothes, make hair and eyewear decisions every couple years, pay attention to your accessories, AND wear makeup you also need to realize that your entire body, sans all the above, is sending a message too. Of course, this is commonly known as body language and can be one of the strongest methods of nonverbal communication. Facial expressions, body posture, and body movements can all send a message about who you are and what your brand is all about.

The good and bad news is that body language is mostly subconscious motor memory. This is good news because once you teach yourself positive muscle memories, like sitting up straight instead of hunching, then your body language will represent your brand automatically. The bad news is that you may have to break some bad habits in order to form better ones. Identifying these habits is the easy part. Breaking them...not so much. To identify bad body language habits, just ask a third party person or watch a video of yourself. A coworker will be able to tell you that you fidget and close off when you talk to the boss. Likewise, simply watching a video of yourself might reveal that your eye contact is flighty and nervous.

It's hard to identify certain body language if you have no idea what you're supposed to look for. For starters, pull out your list of attributes that you would like to be known as (e.g. all that personal branding statement from before). These traits are your end goal, and you need to be on the lookout for any body language that does not support your ideal attributes. Ask a coworker to watch you all day and write down when you are displaying actions that do not align with your personal brand traits. Likewise, you can watch a video of yourself and look for inconsistencies in your movements and how you would like to be perceived. Below are the top characteristics again and what each of those look like (and don't look like!) when it comes to body language.

Articulate. *Adj. 1. Able to express ideas clearly and effectively in speech or writing*

Have you ever been listening to someone talk only to realize that you've been so distracted by their hand gestures, constant leg crossing and uncrossing, and/or room pacing that you haven't actually heard a word they've said? Articulate people speak, write, dress, and- yes- move with purpose. Every motion their body makes seems to serve a purpose. Hand movements emphasize points while they're speaking, head nods provide listening feedback to others, and even walking around the room helps illustrate a concept. Try to take a video of yourself talking with coworkers or friends. Watch the video several times including with and without sound. Do you find yourself making unnecessary and distracting movements or faces? Identify what body language is helpful to the conversation and which is less so. Being mindful of your movements and facial expressions will help you come across as more articulate and purposeful.

Authentic (also: genuine). *Adj. 1. Real or genuine: not copied or false. 2. True and accurate*

Luckily, authentic body language is really easy to master; you simply do nothing. There are two things, however, than can make us seem fake: 1- We lack confidence and are therefore always fidgeting or putting our body in awkward positions and 2- we are trying so hard to control our body movements (for example, trying to break a body language habit) that we look stiff and/or unnatural. Self-affirmations, positive thinking, and even therapy can all help solve problem 1, while practice will take care of any unnatural movements being caused by problem 2.

Competent. *Adj. 1. Having suitable or sufficient skill, knowledge, experience, etc., for some purpose; properly qualified*
It shouldn't surprise you to learn that confident body language can lead people to believe you are competent. Imagine that you get lost in your hotel and end up stumbling into the annual meeting of the Cognitive Neuroscience Society. You are an advertising professional and don't have the slightest clue about neuroscience but you don't want to make a scene so you sit through the last two talks. One talk is given by a man who seems very nervous. He hides behind the lectern reading off his notes, pauses often, and fidgets. The next talk is given by a man who walks confidently up to stage and proceeds to discuss his topic with passion while dominating the entire stage. You have no idea whether either gentlemen said anything of worth or truth, but your brain has already decided which it thinks is more component- the confident man. You brain sees someone who believes in themselves and what they are talking about and, therefore, decides that the person must be credible. If you are having a hard time getting people to view you as competent you need to do the following two things: 1- Assess your work. Do you actually know what you're doing and are you proving it through your words and actions? 2- Assess your appearance. Are you displaying a confidence in yourself and your abilities or is your body language denying your credibility?

Creative. *Adj. 1. Having or showing an ability to make new things or think of new ideas*
Creative people are open to new ideas and your body language needs to reflect that openness. When talking with others, make sure your face is smiling, nodding, and engaging to show that you are friendly and interested. Also make an effort to open your body language by facing the person you're engaging with and uncrossing your arms and legs. Physical openness will signal to the other person or people that you are probably also mentally open. Think of it this way: you want to be seen as a creative, out of the box thinker at your workplace. Are

you going to get that across best by hearing new ideas with a scowl and crossed arms or with a smile and body akimbo?

Dependable *(see also: reliable, trustworthy). Adj. Able to be trusted to do or provide what is needed: able to be depended on*
When it comes to looking dependable, confident body language is the key. If you seem unsure of yourself, then others will be unsure of you too. Stand up straight and tall making sure you don't hunch or slouch, even if you're sitting. Display friendliness by opening up your body (arms and legs uncrossed, shoulders facing the person you're talking to) and smiling. If you really want to create a connection with someone else, mirror their movements. You'll want to do this in the least 'Simons Says' sort of way while still moving your body in the same ways they are moving theirs. Avoid touching your face if at all possible. Also, avoid resting your hand behind your head with your elbow pointed outwards. These are both signs that you are unsure or not at ease.

Funny. *Adj. 1. Causing laughter*
Any comedian knows that being funny is not just about what you say, but also the way you say it and the body language that accompanies the joke. If you're not sure what I'm talking about, watch a comedian perform without the sound on. You'll see that funny people have the eyebrow raises, smirks, and body language that is associated with humor. The biggest problem isn't learning how to use your body to enhance humor, but often times it's how to control your body from being humorous at inappropriate times. Mimicking a funny face your boss makes may make you seem funny, but it could also hurt your career. Understand that your body language is an important resource in joking around and practice using appropriate humor at the right time.

Generous (also: giving) *Adj. 1. Providing more than the amount that is needed or normal: abundant or ample*

Generous people are open to the needs of others. They might also display characteristics of being warm, caring, and emotionally intelligent. Their body language and facial expressions are usually open, friendly, and inviting. These people often have warm, friendly smiles that feel authentic and are great at listening with their entire body (leaning in, head tilted and nodding showing interest and participation, smiling, etc.). They also don't make you feel judged and often avoid closing up their body to you (by means of crossing arms or legs, leaning backwards, facing their feet towards you rather than the exit, etc.). A generous person's body language is going to be similar these traits, elaborated below: intelligent, kind, and loving.

Happy. *Adj. 1. Delighted, pleased, or glad, as over a particular thing*
We all know a happy person when we see one. We often use the terms 'beaming' and 'glowing' to describe those in particularly happy situations like weddings and baby showers. The dead giveaway for happiness is the smile. Experts (yes, there are such things as smile experts) usually identify around six types of smiles ranging from tight-lipped fake smiles to full blown, teeth showing, eyes squinting smiles. In general, the more facial muscles you have engaged during a smile the happier you appear to be. A customer service representative who's had a long day may give you a closed mouth smile without engaging her eyes. This uses far less muscles than the friend you haven't seen in years who greets you excitedly. Aside from genuine (these usually cause small wrinkles on the outsides of your eyes) big smiles, happy people display more relaxed, open body language. When sitting, they are often lounging and seem more laid back. When standing, they often stand akimbo and let their arms either help animate their words or simply let them hang loose by their sides. You never get the feeling that happy people want to be somewhere else. Rather, they always seem like they are enjoying the moment and the people involved.

Independent. *Adj. 1. Not subject to control by others. 2. Not requiring or relying on something else*
People who are secure in their own independence use body language and posture that is confident, and sometimes, bold. They almost never look worried or clingy. The furrowed brow and fidgety hands of a worrier tell others she feels like her life is out of control and going in an unfavorable direction. The woman who won't let go of her friend's arm all night appears insecure and unable to function on her own. Meanwhile, the thriving independent adult is capable of enjoying her own company and is comfortable with or without others. She stands tall, uses her body to support her words, and employs open body language to make others feel welcome in her presence

Intelligent (also: intellectual, emotionally intelligent). *Adj. 1. Having or showing the ability to easily learn or understand things or to deal with new or difficult situations: having or showing a lot of intelligence*
One of the easiest ways to appear intelligent with your body language is to keep your mouth shut. Imagine a child watching television: eyes big and focused on the screen while the mouth hangs open simply swinging on the hinges. This is what you want to avoid. A gaping mouth, even if it's ever so slightly open, will make you look like a dummy. When it comes to the eyes, just the opposite is true. You will look smarter if you keep your eyes open. If you think that's stupid advice, just look at Dr. Ben Carson who ran for president in 2015/6. The general public had trouble thinking Carson was smart enough to handle being president because his eyes were closed to the point where it looked like he was sleeping most the time. Even though he was a skilled neurosurgeon (aka: not an idiot by any stretch of the imagination) he had trouble fighting the assumptions the American public were making because of his closed eyes. So, keep your mouth shut, your eyes open, and then respond to others with verbal or nonverbal feedback to show that you are listening and understanding what they're saying. Non-verbal feedback would include nodding,

smiling, and leaning in while verbal feedback would include saying things like, 'yes', 'I see,'etc.

Kind. (also closely related to loving) *Adj. 1. Of a good or benevolent nature or disposition, as a person*
Have you ever heard the term, 'resting bitch face'? It's used to describe people whose faces appear snobby or malcontent when they aren't actively trying to make them look like anything. Their face simply being their face makes them look unfriendly and judgemental. The faces of kind people have the exact opposite effect. Kind people seem to have perpetually 'resting friendly face'. Much like happiness, the secret to the resting friendly face has to do with the smile. Unlike happiness, however, it's not necessarily about how big the smile can be. Kind smiles are more low-grade. The lips are usually kept shut with no teeth showing, but the eyes still crinkle in true emotion. It's the sort of smile you return to an acquaintance at the grocery store. Nice, friendly, and pleasant but not over enthused (and thus fake looking). You know you're doing it right if random normal people seem to want to talk to you, whether they're asking for directions or just starting up a conversation. I must seem very friendly and at ease when I travel, because I always get stopped by tourists who are lost and looking for guidance. It's as if they scan the subway car looking for a friendly and non-threatening face to ask for help. This common scenario can actually help you on your quest to look more kind. Ask a friend to take several pictures of you throughout the day. Afterwards, look them over and ask yourself, "is this someone I would feel comfortable approaching if I was lost and needed directions?" If the answer is 'no', you may want to work on trading your resting bitch face out for something a bit sweeter.

Loving. *Adj. 1. Feeling or showing love. 2. Very careful and thorough*
It's worth noting that you don't actually have to touch anyone to be seen as loving. While being hands-on does express a certain type of

love, you should be aware that it isn't always appropriate and may make the other party feel uncomfortable. Before we discuss non-touching ways of showing love, let's discuss a few ways to use touch effectively. First of all, if you're at work or an otherwise professional setting keep it very conservative. Okay areas to touch include hands (handshakes) and, as long as contact is 2 seconds or less, shoulders and elbows. If you aren't sure, limit your physical contact to the handshake. All other territory is a no go zone unless you are in a region of the world where other forms of touch are permissible (like a la bise, or cheek kiss, in France).

Like I mentioned, though, you don't have to touch someone to show them you care. Your parents may still show you love even though they don't physically hold you like a child anymore. Likewise, a teacher may seem loving to his/her students without touching them. In order to do this, you have to use your body to pay attention, hence showing respect, to the other person. Easy ways to show you are giving your undivided attention include good eye contact, smiling, leaning in, and head nodding. Positioning your entire body (shoulders, hips, and feet) toward the other person in an open, friendly way will also give the impression that you are solely interested in the person across from you. Next time you're at a cafe or restaurant, watch how different people use their bodies to show interest in the conversation. New couples or close friends chatting excitingly away will probably display the actions I mentioned above while distracted couples or friends will have less engaged body language. Focusing the time and energy to alter your body language in a way that is open and interested shows great amounts of respect, compassion, and love without ever having to touch the other person.

Passionate. *Adj. 1. Having, showing, or expressing strong emotions or beliefs*
Earlier this year, I had the unique opportunity to volunteer my time and talents to coach a Boys and Girls Club Teen in a speech contest. When he got up to do his initial speech, he stated how much he loved

working out and healthy lifestyles, but with no facial or verbal signs of excitement. I figured he either didn't actually care about healthy lifestyles or he was nervous. After working with him for several months I found out that he cares deeply about leading a healthy life, but that he has a serious demeanour. We had to work on using his body language and voice to express his passion while giving the speech. By simply changing his pitch and facial expressions, he was able to get up in front of a large audience at his state finals and successfully convince them that he was passionate about his topic. Generally, when you start talking about something you are passionate about, you talk faster and your voice may change pitches. You usually lean in, your eyes widen, and you may move more than usual (I will start pacing) when you start getting excited about whatever you're talking or hearing about. Your body language is usually open, meaning no crossed arms or legs. Make sure you don't over enthuse your words and actions or you'll come across fake, however, you do want to have a visible energy radiating from you when discussing things you're passionate about.

Professional. *Adj. 1. Relating to a job that requires special education, training, or skill*
Professional posture and body language is pretty straight forward. First of all, make sure your posture is good by standing up tall and straight. Make sure you make eye contact with whomever you're speaking with. Don't stare them down and make them uncomfortable or constantly glance around the room while they're speaking. Try to stay relatively still and avoid fidgeting. Most people have nervous ticks that show their ugly faces whenever the person is anxious, under pressure, or merely concentrating. Ask coworkers what your ticks may be or watch a video of yourself in a high stakes meeting. You may not have cognitively realized that you were an eyebrow puller, pen clicker, or face scratcher type of person until it is revealed to you.

Relatable. Adj. 1. *Being able to establish a social or sympathetic relationship with a person or thing*

Body language can either be dominant, cooperative, or submissive. If you want people to respect you, adapt dominant body language. If you want others to lead you, choose submissive body language. If you want to seem relatable, go for cooperative body language. Cooperative body language means that both parties have equally strong (or weak) actions. In other words, you're either both in strong power poses, both standing akimbo (neutral), or both in relaxed, laid back poses. You're not lording over or cowering beneath someone else; you're working right along with them- which is somewhere they can relate to. You can also be someone they can relate to by subtly mimicking their movements. Once again, you don't want to do this in a creepy way. The key word here is 'subtle'. If Joe crosses his arms, you wait a moment and then cross yours. When he readjusts by uncrossing them, unfolding his legs, and leaning forward you readjust similarly at the same time. If this sounds impossible or, at best, awkward, then do some people watching next time you watch a one-on-one meeting between two individuals. People who are really in sync, like lovers, best friends, or business partners, will likely mirror each other's body language. Meanwhile, casual friends, first time acquaintances, and coworkers might not be as likely to engage in the same mimicking manner.

Just like your clothes, your body language can be altered to help you achieve your goals. Do you want the boss to notice you? Stand up straight and master a great handshake accompanied by a friendly smile. Do you want people to take you seriously? Walk with confidence and adapt power stances rather than hunching at your desk trying to shrink. Do you want to gain more clients? Work on displaying a confident posture and friendly body language that shows you are genuinely interested in them as people as opposed to a pay check.

To start thinking deeper about your body language and how to improve it to reach your goals, I've included an exercise on the following page. During this exercise, you'll start identifying what body language resonates with your personal brand, and prioritize any improvements that need to be made.

BODY LANGUAGE IMPROVEMENT EXERCISE

1. Write out your personal brand statement again:

_____

_____

_____

_____

2. Think of someone or several different people who embody the characteristics in your personal brand statement. Watch their body language and make notes about how they use their body to enforce certain traits (e.g. trustworthiness, friendliness, etc.). Alternatively, you can also choose some of the characteristics outlined in the chapter and write down what body language is indicative of each trait. Make notes here:

_____

_____

_____

_____

3. Now, take a day to be aware of your body and how it reacts to different people and situations. Notice how others react to your body language and posture. Make notes here:

_____

_____

_____

_____

4. Identify inconsistencies between your current body language (#3) and the body language of those who you feel effectively convey the traits you also wish to convey (#2). See the example below to help you get started.

Them: _____Makes good eye contact_____

VS. Me:__Avoids eye contact_____

How I can improve to appear more: _____professional_____

___Focus on making eye contact for at least four second intervals before looking away. Always make eye contact while shaking hands.

Fill in your own here:

Them: _____

VS. Me:_____

How I can improve to appear more: _____

_____

_____

Them: _____

VS. Me:_____

How I can improve to appear more: _____

_____

_____

Them: _____

VS. Me:_____

How I can improve to appear more: _____

_____

_____

5. Write out your mission statement again:

_____

_____

_____

6. Look back over the action items you listed to work on in #4. Will these corrections support your mission statement? You may want to rank them in order of most helpful to least helpful when it comes to your mission statement. Once you've discovered some areas to work on, take one week per item to actively focus on correcting your behavior.

ALL THE LITTLE ADD-ONS

Believe it or not, there is still more that goes into your appearance. Tattoos, piercings, body hair, and hygiene are all important contributors to your image. Depending on your workplace and the way you wish to be perceived, different versions of these things can either hurt or help your career. Visible tattoos would be frowned upon in a lawyer's office, but they are more accepted (and probably much more appreciated) in a music agency. Know what is acceptable in your workplace and what isn't. Also remember, that even though your coworker may have a million piercings and company policy is okay with that, it doesn't necessarily mean that your superior (or anyone else in charge of your upward mobility) is keen on the look. You don't have to change your look for every boss, but you may want to be more cognizant about which tattoos and piercings you choose to display based on your supervisor's preferences. If nothing else, it shows that you respect that person enough to go out of your way to make them more comfortable. Sometimes, it's better to focus on respecting others than parading your own beliefs and opinions about.

RACISM, INTOLERANCE, AND SOCIAL INJUSTICE

It makes sense to change some aspects of our image in order to be perceived a certain way. We cover up tattoos, dress professionally, and sit up straight during job interviews in order to impress others. But, what if the things that are being judged aren't changeable? What if people are perceiving us a certain way because of our skin tone? Or because of a certain type of dress that is important to our religion. What if we do everything we're 'supposed' to do in an interview to be denied a position due to race or religion? I want to specifically address race and religion because those are the two biggest areas of image intolerance in the United States today.

Before I go further, I would like to add a disclaimer. I can not fully understand or comprehend the racism and intolerance that many people in this country and around the world face on a daily basis. As a Caucasian Christian, I am in the majority. In many ways, I am unable to sympathize with those who are judged negatively because of their skin color and religion, however, I do make every effort to be empathetic. I also realize that I cannot solve all the problems of modern day society including racism and religious intolerance, but I do feel like these are topics worth discussing because they are a matter of image intolerance.

Race

Unfortunately, racism is alive and well in this country. The specific race being discriminated against may vary depending on region of the country, city, and even neighborhood. If you are the victim of racial discrimination, I don't have to tell you, you already know it. What I can tell you, though, is how to change your appearance to fight back against racism. It's worth noting that this advice is the same for any group of people that are being stereotyped.

There are two main ways to fight against racism: your actions and your appearance. Negative stereotypes are the foundation for racism. If you can use your actions and your appearance to go against those negative stereotypes, then you are well on your way to making a major change in the world. You should be proud of your ethnicity and never try to conform to someone else's expectations. While you can't (and shouldn't!) change your skin color, you can fight against the unfair and untrue stereotypes that are made about you by actively countering them in how you carry yourself and treat others.

Your appearance specifically, can be an effective tool in the fight against racism and negative stereotypes. Think back to the Civil Rights Movement. There were two main forces within the Civil Rights Movement and they used radically different tactics. On one hand, you had Martin Luther King Jr. leading peaceful protests all across the South. On the other hand, you had the Black Panthers who integrated more aggressive tactics to gain racial equality. Two different methods of handling racism, and also, two very different ways of dressing. Look up any MLK protests and you'll see men and women wearing suits, and often times, their Sunday best. Their clothes were saying, "I am dignified; I am to be respected; I am protesting in peace." The Black Panthers chose an entirely different way of dressing. Instead of suits, they chose leather jackets and berets. Black leather jackets gave the impression of toughness, which reflected their 'we're not going to take this anymore' attitude, while the berets were inspired by a film founders Huey Newton and Bobby Seale watched about the French resistance of the Nazis. Both parties successfully use their clothing to convey exactly what their mission and tactics were all about.

No matter what your ethnicity, the key is that there is no right or wrong way to dress. Remember, your personal brand is your responsibility to convey. Be deliberate in how you dress, how you carry yourself, and how you communicate.

Religion

The more aware you are of the stereotypes facing your race, the more able you are to make conscious decisions against them. This is true for any negative stereotype including religion. Just like race, different religious groups are also discriminated against in different regions of the country, cities, and neighborhoods. I'll specifically talk about Islam, because Muslims are commonly victims of discrimination in today's society.

Unfortunately for Muslims, religious extremists have created the unjust stereotype that anyone who is Arabic or practices Islam is a terrorist. This is a double whammy for people of Arabic ethnicity who are Muslim because they are getting speared with both racism and religious intolerance. Equally horrible, is that it's much harder for Muslims to fight back against their stereotypes than other discriminated parties. Think about it. Women are often negatively stereotyped as inferior with tools and fixing things. Muslims are negatively stereotyped as terrorists. It's a lot easier for me to install my own ceiling fan and defy my stereotype than it is for an Arabic person or Muslim to defend that they aren't a terrorist. If you really think about it for a minute, it's such a ridiculous thing to defend, that you probably wouldn't know where to start. You can't simply pick up a power drill and prove someone wrong. Meanwhile, all taking your hijab off is going to do is make ignorant people feel more comfortable while compromising your own beliefs, which is a lose-lose situation. So, what do you do?

First, let's start with what you don't do. No matter what religion you are, don't change your beliefs to 'fit in'. If your religion is a defining part of who you are, then be proud of it and don't alter it for anyone else. With that said, the extent to which you display your religious beliefs through your dress is up to you. If I feel the need to let everyone know that I am a Christian, I may decide to wear religious themed jewelry or clothing. I may also dress in a different, more modest manner that reflects my beliefs about conservative dressing. Or, maybe I don't really care about translating my religion through my appearance and, as a result, there is nothing distinctive about what I wear. Regardless of what extent I chose to display or not display my beliefs through my appearance, I have that choice. You will also need to make that choice, and if you choose to be visually apparent about your religion, you'll need to be emotionally and mentally prepared for enquiries at best, and aggression at worst.

Later on, I discuss the delicate balance of staying true to yourself and also respecting others, but I think there's value in touching on it briefly now. I have heard arguments that some religious dress makes people uncomfortable, and the wearer should, therefore dress differently to 'respect others'. To be clear, there is nothing respectful about telling others to change or go against their religious beliefs so that you can stay in your comfort zone. You have to give respect to earn respect. There's also a big difference between verbally proselytizing your religion to everyone you see and simply wearing a religious specific garment. Verbally crossing boundaries and sharing your beliefs where they are not requested or welcomed is disrespectful. Dressing in a way that is in line with your religious beliefs is not disrespectful. If you chose to prominently display your religion through your clothing, take a minute to also assess your words and actions to make sure any religious attributes are reflected appropriately in your personal brand.

Physical Disabilities or Deformations

I've read a countless number of books about appearance, image, and personal branding, and very few, if any, specifically talk about people with physical disabilities and deformities. I can only imagine how frustrating it must be for, say, someone in a wheelchair or a person who requires specific shoes for walking to read everything in this chapter and try to apply it. If you are reading this, and thinking 'yes, that's me!' this is for you.

Just like anyone else, you need to find out how people perceive you and then you can start altering your appearance to bridge the gap between current characteristics and ideal traits. The biggest problem you are going to face is probably being relatable. Most people couldn't begin to relate to a different lifestyle than their own, however, almost everyone is curious. If you can come off as approachable, then people will be more likely to interact with you and hopefully you can start a discussion about how your life isn't that far off from theirs. The process of getting the elephant out of the room, so to speak, can actually help you display parts of your character (resiliency, work ethic, confrontation) and gain trust with your audience.

Another barrier may be confidence. Remember, don't let anything hold you back from becoming the person you wish to become. You may not physically be able to become a professional athlete, but just remember that almost all personal branding characteristics have to do with your character, NOT your physical abilities. Focus on those character traits that you would like to be known for and remind yourself of your end goals. Lack of confidence is one of the biggest barriers to success that anyone can face. Believe in yourself, respect yourself, and make sure you look like you do both of those things. If your appearance radiates a confidence (not arrogance), others are more likely to assume that you are indeed confident and capable.

Personal branding is all about identifying what makes you special and outstanding. While your disability/deformity doesn't define you, it does shape you and it can be a powerful tool in shaping your personal brand. Give some thought as to how you could use your disability/deformity to the greatest advantage. We've all been dealt cards; your cards are just a little different than the person's next to you. Decide which cards will help you be most successful in achieving your mission statement and align your thoughts, actions, and image to reflect your winning hand.

Chapter 3:

Dress your way to a more successful career

Between how you are perceived by others and the psychological effect of what you wear, your appearance is a significant part of your career. Many people focus so much on getting the job done that they forget about the message they are sending in the process. Or, they only pay attention to their appearance during the interview, and after the first week of work, caring for the way they look is all but out the window. Ironically, many of those same people that understand why the student mentioned in the introduction of the book can't rely just on their grades to get a job don't realize that work ethic alone can't guarantee career success. Landing a job and then turning it into a thriving career are things that can't be done simply by having book smarts or being a great people person or looking the part. Rather, you need a combination of talent, charm, grit, and looks to conquer the working world. If the thought of checking off all those boxes gets you nervous, don't be. Simply think of it as being well rounded and living out your personal brand in the workplace.

NAILING THE JOB YOU WANT

Obtaining a fulfilling career is much more complex than simply filling out an application and showing up to an interview. Rather, it's usually the long term result of working many jobs. The key is to get your foot in the door with a basic job in your field and then work your way up. The beginning job may not be glamorous, but it's your first impression in a company, and like all first impressions it's very important. During the job hunting process and throughout the beginning of your career, your image is also quite important. It's what secures you a spot at the table and it's what gives you the ability to move to the head of the table.

Before you get all excited about moving up in a company, you need to actually find a company to work for. As you research different organizations and search through job listings, ask yourself how well the mission of each company matches up with your own personal brand and mission. Are your values and priorities similar? The majority of people I talk to that don't like their jobs are either a bad fit with their employer or simply don't want to work. While I can't help you much with that last issue, I can offer some advice on the former. Don't neglect the research part of your job search. Actually make an effort to learn about the company and find out from others if you would be a good fit. With that said, you have to be realistic. I have known many a recent college graduate who live at home for months while they search for 'the perfect job'. They turn down job offers for positions that they feel are beneath them, when in fact, they are not qualified for anything more than entry level positions. You can share the same values as a company and still work an entry level job that you're not crazy about. The important part is that you're working in a company that you care about and you are working towards a mission that you believe in. Setting a foundation like that will help you as you move forward in the same company or grow into a different organization.

Once you find a company that you can stand behind, you need to get in the door. If they don't have any current job openings, do some reconnaissance and find any common connections you have with people that work there. You might have to network your way in. If there are job openings, put your name in the hat. And by 'put your name in the hat' I mean, go out of your way to do everything possible to make the absolute best first impression you can. Seriously. Blow them out of the water. You want to be a candidate that is so desirable that they feel they should snatch you up before someone else does. Write a killer cover letter, tailor your resume, and make them feel like they are the greatest company on Earth. You don't need to get creepy or annoying. Instead, just imagine yourself in their HR department's shoes. What kind of person would you hire? Who would you want on your team? What qualities would that person have and what kind of application would blow you out of the water? That's what you need to hone in on.

While many applications are filled out and filed entirely online these days, it is best to show your face whenever possible. Most jobs get lots of applications and it's very easy to become just another name on a list. One of the easiest ways to prevent falling between the cracks (other than having stellar application) is to give human resources a visual to associate with a name. If you have the opportunity to turn in an application in person do it. A name with a face is vital to getting you to the final round. It's, of course, best if the face accompanying the name is atop a well-dressed and groomed body. Somebody who looks like they are on top of their game and looks like they would fit into the company is remembered in a very positive light.

For a brief time, I was the manager of small, independently owned pet store. As the store manager, I was in charge of all hiring duties including job postings, application screening, interviews, and hiring paperwork. This particular store was located in rural western New York State where unemployment was very high. We rarely went more than two days in a row without someone coming in to ask for an application. We had so many people, in fact, that I stopped buying the generic application forms and simply instructed my employees to say, "We aren't hiring right now (yes, all these people simply wandered into the store asking for jobs, not because there was any sort of job posting) but if you'd like to bring us a resume, we'll keep it on file and that's the first thing the manager looks at when she is ready to hire someone new." That was the truth too. If you cared enough to actually bring me a resume then you would probably care enough to show up to work on time and actually be a good employee. Over the course of a year, I only received 10 resumes. Worse than that, was the way people presented themselves to ask for applications (the worst dressers never brought in resumes). I saw men in undershirts and sweatpants sagging below their butts, women in shirts revealing more breast or stomach than I ever wanted to see, and lots of yoga pants and flip flops. It still amazes me to think that someone would ever walk into a store and think that they would get hired wearing an oversized t-shirt and leggings. They may not be coming in for an interview, but they don't know who the manager is and I was almost always watching. The funny thing was that these weren't genuinely poor people who truly couldn't afford anything to wear. The same people who asked for jobs wearing dirty clothes five sizes too small would not hesitate to drop $150 on a new ferret. The point here is to look your best, even if you are just picking up an application or dropping it off. You never know who's looking. I interviewed a candidate purely because he showed up in a button down shirt and tie. I also made sure to give him lots of positive feedback about his outfit and to keep looking his best for every job interview from then on.

You may think that an interview is your first impression, when it really might not be. When I saw applicants who didn't care enough to change out of pajamas in order to ask for a job, I made a note of it on their application. Always look your best even if you are going to the jiffy store around the corner from the company. You never know who will be in there picking up a midday snack and making notice of you.

While we may not always think about looking our best for picking up/dropping off an application, most of us know to look decent during an interview. Dressing for an interview usually involves generic advice like 'wear a dark, conservative colored suit' and 'cut your fingernails'. In reality, what is appropriate to wear to an interview varies depending on the industry, job being applied for, and even the time of year.

The best way to know what is appropriate for your situation is to reference what current employees are wearing. In the least creepy way possible (you don't want to make a bad impression), try to figure out what the dress code is like. Maybe you sit at the coffee shop across the street in the morning when everyone is filing into the building. Or perhaps you drive by the building at the end of the day when everyone is getting off work. Try to be at least a little suave about it; don't just park your car in the organization's front drive and stare. Also make an effort to look your best. If the hiring manager, CEO, or anyone in between sees you, you want them to remember you as the sharp looking guy in the coffee shop and not the rough looking guy creeping outside their building. While you're watching employees stream in and out of the building note everything you can about their appearance. What clothes are they wearing? What about their shoe wear? Do they show tattoos or wear casual clothing? You want to aim for the level of formality they are wearing and then kick it up a notch. For example, if the employees are wearing mostly jeans and t-shirts, then plan on wearing khakis and a blazer. You want to look polished and professional, but not overdressed to the point that you look like a sore thumb. Your goal is a look that is respectful and relatable so that everyone who sees you will think, "He looks like he would fit in here."

If you aren't able to easily observe company employees, or still aren't sure about what to wear you'll have to resort to different methods. If you applied online, you may not have to look any further than the company's website. The career page of most websites will have some sort of picture. More often than not, the picture is usually something like candidates at a job fair, or a group of new recruits. These pictures were specifically chosen by the company to display what they feel the ideal candidate looks like, so use them as your guide! Are the recruits wearing black suits with slicked back hairstyles? Or are they wearing jeans and polo shirts? This will give you an idea of what that particular organization is looking for. If the company doesn't have a job section of its website, you can always research competitor companies, because they will most likely be looking for similar candidates.

Somewhere, sometime, someone thought it was a good idea to tell job seekers that it was okay to call human resources and ask about appropriate interview attire. This advice makes me cringe in the worst way possible. I hate it so much, because it comes across that you are not resourceful or motivated enough to try to figure out the answer on your own. Instead, you play the easy card and take up someone else's time. The only time I can even fathom this being appropriate is if the interview is very non-traditional, like a picnic at a State Park. But even then, you should be able to use some deductive reasoning and come up with something casual, yet refined. Calling the HR manager to verify your wardrobe choices should definitely be an absolute last resort.

When it comes to interview dressing, every industry plays by different rules. Here are some general interview outfit tips for several popular industries.

Professional Services (law, insurance, finance, management, etc.)

These careers tend toward more serious dressing. If you're going to be in charge of someone's mortgage, divorce settlement, retirement money, or a whole department of people, you need to look mature and responsible. This isn't the time to show your creative side or parade around your favorite cat sweater. You'll want to stick with dark, conservative suits paired with power colors. Now is the time to pull out that red tie, or purple blouse. Skip the pastels (save from baby blue men's button down shirts), greens, and pinks. Wear yellows or blues if you need to come across as cheerful or loyal, respectively. All tattoos should be covered and any piercings more than one hole in each ear for females, should be removed. Jewelry should be conservative and tasteful; keep it small and classy. Purses, briefcases, and shoes should all be well taken care of and polished (when applicable). Men should wear dress shoes, while women should wear closed toe shoes less than 2 inches in height. Hair should be well groomed and pulled back from the face. Men should be clean shaven. While it may seem very conservative, remember that in this industry, the workplace is not the time to stretch your sartorial wings.

Creative Services (advertising, marketing, design, writing, fashion, etc.)

Stepping outside that conservative, dark suit territory will probably help you, however, if you are applying for a creative job. Human Resource professionals want someone who will be able to think creatively and solve problems outside the box. Your work history, the words coming out of your mouth, and your very appearance should all verify your abilities to do just that. Having said that, don't go crazy. You don't want to come across as someone who, at worst, is so eccentric they'd have trouble getting along with others or is, at best, just a complete weirdo. You can usually get away with trendier outfits as long as they are still polished and professional. For example, fitted ankle pants with a tuxedo blazer and white button down shirt would make for an appropriate fashion interview outfit, but would be inappropriate for a wealth management interview. A good rule of thumb is to stick to one statement piece per outfit. A fun necklace over a black shift dress or a printed pencil skirt with a classic blouse are more than enough variance in your ensemble to tell others that you are a creative thinker. Muted colors and geometric prints always read as more expensive and classy than bright colors and playful prints. Shoes should still be closed toe and, for the ladies, shorter than 2 inches in height. Hair should be clean and all facial hair should be well groomed. All parts of your appearance (including hair and eyewear) should read as current and up to date. No one will want to hire a marketing guy that looks like they're stuck in another decade.

Sales (customer service, direct sales, b2b, etc.)

Sales is a tricky industry to generalize because it really depends on what you're selling. What you'd wear to a car dealership interview you would most certainly not wear to a craft brew sales distributor position. The key to dressing for a sales interview is to look professional, serious about the position, and most importantly: authentic. No one wants to hire someone that looks like they'll slack off at their job and who comes across as fake. People who are truly into the product that they are selling usually look that way. The craft brew enthusiast may have a meaningful sleeve of tattoos and a handlebar mustache, but his look embodies the brand of the beer. Likewise, a perfectly suited woman complete with designer heels and french roll looks the part of a high end women's department store. Despite what you're selling, you still need to come across as respectful and professional. You need to look like you take the business and the product seriously. Choosing an outfit that is clean, pressed and reflective of the company (remember to look a step nicer than position you're applying for) is best. Stay away from anything flashy, loud, or cheap looking. Unless you're applying for a job at Hooters and are specifically told to look cheap... keep the halters, tight pants, and sky high heels at home. Men, even if they tell you it's a t-shirt and jeans environment, keep it classy and opt for a polo shirt and tailored jeans.

Administrative Positions + Uniform jobs (front desk, office work, etc.)

Dressing for an administrative or uniformed position falls somewhere between the professional services and sales dressing advice. You need to look sharp, efficient, and capable, but you can kind of let loose a bit- especially if doing so fits in with the company image. A suit is a good place to start, but depending on the formality of the company culture, you can dress that down with your accessories or by mixing and matching suit separates. You don't necessarily need to look like you are preparing to run the company, but you do need to look like someone that can make a good first impression on customers and be capable of handling day to day functions with ease. A casual suit with a knit shell or sweater underneath, printed scarf, and fun (closed toe!) flats would be a great outfit for a woman. A casual suit with pinstriped shirt and colorful pocket square is a good choice for a man. (A casual suit is less formal than your standard black suit. Casual suits may be different colors, materials, or may be trendier than your typical black business suit.) These outfits are professional, but also memorable and a colorful accent will help you stand out in a sea of candidates. If you are applying for a front desk job of some sort, make sure you look your absolute best. This is a job when first impressions weigh heavier than anytime else. You will be the first thing that a customer sees in relation to your company, so it's vital that you look the part and make a stellar first impression.

Regardless of the industry or job position, some things remain consistent. Hair should always be well groomed. Nails should be short, well groomed, and either devoid of color, or with a light neutral polish. Extreme fashions and hairstyles should be avoided. You overall image should be professional, competent, and pulled together. Remember, you're trying to get hired for a job, not go on stage to a Lady Gaga concert, so keep it toned down while still giving them a little flavor of yourself. Your goal when you leave the interview is to keep them wanting more.

You did your research when it came to picking a job to apply for, so don't skimp when it comes to researching what to wear for the interview. Whether it's your first job or fourteenth, do your homework and find out what is appropriate and expected for the company you're interviewing with, then aim to dress a notch higher. The better you're able to channel the company's brand through your outfit, the more likely the interviewer is to see you as someone that would fit in perfectly at their organization....which is exactly what you want.

CLIMBING THE LADDER- NO ATHLETIC SHOES REQUIRED

There is a major misconception among many that you only need to 'dress to impress' during interview and the first week or two on the job. These are the same people that claim their accomplishments at work should be the single deciding factor in their career mobility. Unfortunately, at least for them, that's not the case. What you wear at work matters and it plays a bigger role in succeeding at your career than you think. Here are the top three reasons why:

The higher up you are in a company, the more your appearance matters

This isn't always the case, but it holds true most of the time. Just think about it- a CEO is seen by the public (specifically, as a representative of the company) much more often than a call center employee. If your CEO looks unshaven, tired, and bedraggled it's going to reflect much more poorly on the company than if a call center employee looks like they're having a rough day. Ideally, everyone in the company would look like a perfectly poised representation of a successfully thriving company, but we all know that it doesn't always play out like that. If you want to move up in a company, you have to be prepared to have more eyes on you. And, of course, the more people watching you, the more important it is that you look like a leader. When it comes to making a decision about moving someone up in the company, a person's self-presentation is actually quite important. If you have any number of employees working under that person, they should be able to lead, not only with their words and actions, but with their appearance. A manager will have no credit with employees if he is telling them to act professional, yet he fails to look the part. If you are performing your job above expectations and people less qualified than you are receiving promotions you think you deserve, take a hard look at your appearance. It may be the reason you are being held in the back office away from customers or being overlooked when it comes time to promote within.

Your appearance affects the way others perceive you

Despite what message your performance is sending (look at all these reports; she's such a hard worker!), others may be making judgements about your overall abilities based on your appearance. In fact, those other people may not even realize that they are forming opinions about your work ethic and skill level based on what you look like. So many of our decisions and opinions are influenced by all the information we take in around us subconsciously. This is one of the many reasons why it's vital that your appearance and body language reflect your personal brand. When your image backs up your actions, you will be viewed as a more trustworthy person. According to studies, when people make first impressions, they are either judging for credibility or trustworthiness. Credibility is nice, but it's really the trustworthy factor that leads to successful networking, better business partnerships, and long lasting relationships. Look the way you wish to be perceived, and you'll have already won half the battle. Just the other day I was at the pharmacy picking up some medicine for my husband. The pharmacy tech helping me had an unkempt appearance (wrinkled, half unbuttoned shirt, sloppy fitting pants, and wildly unmaintained hair) and a general facial expression of displeasure. As she was ringing me up, I was carefully watching the screen to make sure she didn't charge me incorrectly. Subconsciously, I had made a connection between her appearance and her abilities- if one was careless, then the other must be also. As the transaction went on, her unhappy face became friendly and chatty, which helped regain my trust in her abilities. The experience ended up being pleasant and error-free. It was only after reflecting on the transaction that I realized how much I was affected by the tech's appearance and body language. Every day we are constantly making decisions based on how we perceive others, so let's not forget to be extra aware of how others are perceiving us!

Your image affects the quality of your work

In 2011 and 2012, Northwestern University's Kellogg School of Management led a series of studies testing if and how participants were affected by different clothes. In the first study, participants were asked to wear either a white lab coat or their street clothes, and then tested for their ability to spot errors. Participants wearing the white lab coats, similar to physician's coats, made half as many mistakes as those who didn't. The researchers then went on to perform two more studies, which we'll discuss later. While it's not known if the results of your clothing on your psyche are long lasting, there is definitely an association between dress and action. Simply the role of dressing for a certain part (whether that's putting on a lifeguard uniform or a suit for the office) can help us mentally prepare to function in that role. It can also give us the confidence to perform our duties to the fullness of our job description.

WHY OFF CLOCK DRESSING STILL MATTERS

What you wear outside of work can affect your career. I know what you're thinking (besides...will she ever just give me a break?) You've worked hard to separate your home life and your work life and it seems unfair that one should still dictate the other- even when it comes to something as basic as clothing. My short response to that is, 'yes, it is unfair and yes, it does matter.'

For one, you never know who you will run into outside the office and every moment is a first impression. Your future boss could be behind you in the Walgreens line (skeptically eyeing your t-shirt covered in weed leaves). Your next big client might bump into you at the grocery store or the dog park. Wherever you are, you need to be on your game- appearance included. One easy way to keep your look sharp is to assess your outfit before leaving the house and ask yourself, "If someone asks me what I do, wherever I am going today, and I told them my mission statement or personal brand would they think, 'oh yeah, I can see that!', or 'hmmm, that's interesting' (aka: there's a disconnect and I'm having trouble believing you are what you say you are)." Whether you're headed to the drugstore, board meeting, or your kid's soccer game, asking that question will ensure that you are properly dressed to impress.

Does that mean you should wear a suit every time you go to CVS or to sit on the bleachers for an athletic event? Of course not. That would impractical and, quite honestly, a little weird. Instead, you need to figure out how to translate your personal brand into casual weekend wear. A professionally polished look for errands might include tailored dark wash jeans and a pressed oxford or fitted t-shirt with a fun scarf. A creative, detail oriented brand might manifest itself by means of tailored chinos, fun socks, coordinating boat shoes and belt, and a locally designed t-shirt. Think about your fashion icon who embodies the ideal personal brand (in your eyes). What would they wear on their time off? If you admire Oprah Winfrey's personal brand, imagine what she would wear on a trip to the grocery store or Starbucks. Use that as inspiration to ramp up your own outside-of-work game.

Opportunities are everywhere, and you never know when a happenstance meeting will prove beneficial to you personally or professionally. You don't even need to have an interaction with anyone to have your appearance work in your favor. Someone may see, process, and make an assumption about you without you even knowing it! Think about it. Can you identify all the people who saw you in Walmart last weekend? Of course not; no one could do that. But just because you didn't take note of others doesn't mean that they didn't take note (and form a first impression) of you.

No matter where you are or what you're doing, you need to be making a stellar first impression. In order to make this easier for myself (because who wants to stress out every time they leave the house for any little thing?), I have outfits mentally picked out for errand running. These are my go-to outfits that ensure that I look exactly the way I wish to be perceived. Dark wash jeans from J.Crew, button down oxfords from Ralph Lauren, and fun flats make up my errand running outfit list. Scarves, jewelry, and blazers are added when I feel like spicing it up (or thinking). In the winter, the outfit is very similar, except I pair the jeans with riding boots and add a cashmere sweater. If you have a couple basic outfits on rotation, you will never be tempted to leave the house wearing anything less than your best! If you are tempted to always grab the sweatpants and hoodie before heading outside, I recommend keeping your lounge clothing in a drawer labeled lounge clothing. This visually reinforces that some clothes are meant for lounging at home while others are meant for the real world.

A year or two ago, during a minor lack of judgement, I bought my husband a puppy for Christmas. My availability was much better than my husbands, seeing as I worked from a home office, so taking the dog out during the day became one of my responsibilities. During the whole potty training time, I lived in Iowa, which to say the least can get quite chilly in the winters and I was prone to leave the house in long underwear more often than I'd like to admit. One such day, I was at the dog park looking less than my best in a desperate attempt to keep warm and keep up with a dog when a fellow dog owner started up a conversation. It didn't take long for her to ask the age old question, 'so what do you do?' when I realized with great embarrassment that I couldn't tell her I was an image consultant looking the way I did. Instead, I mumbled something about consulting and changed the subject. Great impression right? Chances are that nothing would have ever become of the interaction, even if I was dressed impeccably. However, I can't help but wonder what great stories, business opportunities, or networking I denied myself by not looking my best.

YOUR THIRD IDENTITY- THE ONLINE WORLD

If it wasn't enough to adequately convey your personal brand at work and outside work, you also need to make sure it's consistent with your online image. Interviews have been denied and employees have been fired for showing less than their best (or maybe too much of 'their best') online. When it comes to the great interwebs, just remember, anyone can see almost anything. If your boss isn't friends with you on Facebook, that doesn't mean that your profile picture doesn't pop up in his feed (do you know this person?) or on his wife's feed (who just so happens to be friends with your neighbor). Don't take the chance of ruining your reputation by posting comments and pictures that don't reflect how you wish to be perceived. A good rule of thumb I personally use is not to post anything that I wouldn't show to my grandmother.

While it's better to have no online presence than a bad online presence, it's not entirely a good thing to be invisible on the internet. In today's day and age, if you don't exist online, you don't exist. Try googling yourself. What comes up? Look at the hits that actually have to do with you (this can be tricky if you have a common name) and ask yourself, "do these results reflect my personal brand?" If someone who didn't know you at all, like say a hiring recruiter, looked up your name, would they see your best attributes displayed? Would they see articles written about you on your expertise, or accolades from the latest newspaper, or an award listed on the company website? You don't have to be everywhere, but you should have at least a page, depending on your age and length of time in your career, of impressive results that will surely wow any HR manager or future client.

Here are several places that your name could (or should) pop up across the World Wide Web:

Social Media Sites
Social Media Sites include, but are not limited to: Facebook, LinkedIn, Twitter, Google+, Snap Chat, Instagram, Tumblr, YouTube, Reddit, Pinterest, Meetup...
I briefly mentioned that, as a good rule of thumb, I don't post anything on any of these sites that I wouldn't want my grandmother to see. The reason for that is way more than just the fact that my grandmother is actually on Facebook as sees everything I do. Social

media sites give third party observers a glance into what our non-work lives are all about. Have you ever heard someone comment after browsing through a person's professional website, "ok, let's find them on Facebook and see what they're really like"? It happens all the time. We often let our guard down on social media because we think only our friends are watching and, after all, we have all the right security measures in place right? Not always. An anonymous woman in Switzerland was fired after she called in sick to work with migraines and then spent the day actively using Facebook. I've said it before and I'll say it again: successful people use every tool they can possibly get their hands on to become even more successful. Any social media site can be a tool for success if you use it properly.

Websites

Websites may include: personal websites, blogs, organization websites, and company websites.

If you Google my name, 'Leslie Friedman', you will see my personal website. At different times in my life, you would also have seen my name and photo on organization's websites that I've been involved in and different blogs I've authored. These are all prime ways to connect your personal brand with your name and face. The best part about websites is that you have a lot of control over what is published. If it's your own personal website or blog, then you have complete control over how the entire world via the internet sees you. Take a moment to look through your personal websites and blogs and ask yourself if what you see on those websites reflects your personal brand statement and/or mission statement. If they're not in sync, figure out what necessary changes need to be made.

When it comes to the websites of different organizations, focus your time on the organizations that reflect the same values and interests of your personal brand. I may be a board member on my Homeowner's Association Board and my local Health Clinic Board. If I am a physician in the area, I would focus on making sure the description and headshot on the Health Clinic's website is more visible and up-to-date than the HOA. Don't forget that many organizations put their minutes online and a simple search for your name can pull up all sorts of information from meeting notes. It may be worth asking organizations you're involved with, what information is published online and what isn't. Obviously, you could also find this information by doing some sleuthing about on the web.

Last, you have company websites. Have you ever started a new job and had Human Resources take a quick picture of you from day one only to find it used in all the company's PR (Look at our new marketing assistant!)? Make sure you're prepared with a short bio that reflects your personal brand statement in case HR decides to do some public relations work. You can also volunteer your own headshot instead of being subjected to a makeshift one taken by a HR assistant and not a photographer. Remember, it never hurts to ask, and most HR professionals will gladly accept both a well-written bio and a nice headshot, as it saves them some work.

Online Media

Online media consists of: newspaper articles, media interviews, featured online articles, company announcements, press releases, and other public relation materials written about you.

Out of the three categories, this is the one we probably have the least control over. While I think Donald Trump has somewhat proven the theory that 'any press is good press', it's worth avoiding bad press if at all possible. If you know you are going to be interviewed for the media, make sure you've properly rehearsed any possible questions you might be asked. Additionally, make sure the answers you've come up with support your personal brand statement. This is true whether you are doing an interview for a local TV station or are guest blogging on the Wall Street Journal. If your name is associated with a press release or some other written media material, take the time to review the document and (are you ready for this?) check it for inconsistencies with your mission statement. Remember, people who are household names in their fields didn't just become who they are today by accident. Rather, it is an ongoing process of deliberately reassuring that anything anyone sees about you is consistent with how you want to be seen. If bad press does surface about you, you can attempt to get rid of it, or you can work with the SEO (search engine optimization) of other sites, like your own, to ensure that it doesn't land on the first three pages of google results when your name is searched.

All three parts of the internet have several things in common including a profile picture or headshot. Headshots or profile pictures are the internet's version of first impressions and are vital. For this reason, I'm going to delve a little deeper into why they are important and how you can make the perfect one.

I've seen a lot of really good headshots and an equal amount of really bad ones. While your headshot may be mainly used for interior purposes at your company, it may also be displayed on the company website, etc. If you are someone whose face will be plastered on the company page and beyond, it's imperative that your picture is sending the right message.

It's actually harder to create a positive first impression with a picture than in person. This is due to several factors: the viewer can stare at the picture without negative social implications, the viewer doesn't feel emotionally attached to the person in the picture and will judge more harshly, and the person in the picture can't say anything to vouch for themselves. Instead, a first impression is created just based on lighting, clothing choice, hairstyle, and makeup. On the positive side, you can use any of those items in your favor to create a photo that looks exactly the way you wish to be perceived.

Your headshot should be taken by a professional who knows what he's doing. Describe to him how you wish to look. Maybe you want to seem friendly and inviting. Maybe you want to look serious and responsible. A good photographer should be able to dictate your position and facial expression to achieve the look you want. I suggest looking through headshots to find ones that you feel are particularly strong and that convey the message you wish to send. Show these examples to the photographer and explain exactly what you like about each one. This will help ensure that your online first impression is sending the right message.

You may want to consider having several different headshots or photos for different online avenues. While you can use the same generic headshot for Facebook, LinkedIn, and your company website, it may be better to switch things up to reflect the personality of the website or social media account. For example, you would want a more serious looking headshot for LinkedIn and a corporate website than you might for your YouTube channel or your Instagram account. Sometimes, depending on what you do, you might need different headshots for different websites. I once had a client who had two very different businesses, a healthcare facility and a pet care business, and she used two very different pictures of herself with each one. The healthcare facility website showed her in a medical outfit with a basic black backdrop. It was professional and appropriate for healthcare. Meanwhile, she chose a relaxed picture of her with her animals (that was also taken by a professional) to display on her pet business site. By altering the pictures she showed on each website, she was able to relate to potential clients and gain their respect. The main goals of a headshot or profile picture is to gain trust, credibility, and help the viewer relate to you. Look across your profile pictures and ask yourself, "what message am I sending with this picture", "Is it a message that supports my personal brand?", and, "Does this picture garner trust and respect?"

Chapter 4:
Home is where the happiness grows

A strong personal brand will positively affect much more than just your career. In fact, we need for our brands to continue to stretch across our home and personal lives to benefit those around us. At some point or another, we've probably all encountered the parent who expends all of their energy at work only to come home tired and offering their third or fourth best to the ones they love the most. There's no simple solution to solve the problems of a parent doing it all, but there are several ways we can streamline our lives to make them easier, more productive, and truer to us.

Have you ever walked into someone's home and thought, "wow, there's no mistaking that this is Cindy's house...it looks like her!" Or maybe you've thought the exact opposite ("I never imagined that Kathy would live somewhere like here"). We don't think about it very often, but our homes are extensions of ourselves. When I got married and jumped face first into decorating our first apartment, people would comment on my 'nesting' activities. Even though I wasn't crazy about the term nesting (What am I? A bird about to lay eggs?), I was creating our little personal space that reflected the things most valuable to us. We have an innate desire to make our surroundings reflect our priorities and values, which is why there are so many decorating styles. In this chapter, we'll talk about the effect of your personal brand in the home, and in the people you share your nest with.

HOME AS AN EXTENSION OF SELF

While home decoration is often chucked up to women, both men and women reflect their personal brands equally onto their personal space. Just because a home isn't decorated in the formal sense, doesn't mean that the resident's personality isn't present. Someone with a sloppy abode full of second hand furniture may be thought of as lazy, creative, and/or frugal. Meanwhile, someone who has a pristine home that is stylishly decorated may be seen as concerned about what others think, detail oriented, or Type A. If you're sitting in your home right now, take a minute to look around. What does your home say about you? It's hard to look at something so personal objectively, but imagine that you are a new friend walking into your home for the first time. Would that person see a connection between your brand (or, the person they know you as) and your space? If someone who doesn't know you looked at a picture of a random room in your house and then was given the list of 3-5 attributes you defined as your personal brand...would they think the two aligned?

Having a personal brand that doesn't flow into the way your home looks isn't detrimental. To my knowledge, no one has died from a misaligned career/home personal brand. It's not something that is going to create immediate turmoil, but it is going to wear you down over time rather than building you up. Office buildings provide a great example of this. Think of your basic office building; perhaps even the one you might work in. Visions of cubicles, water stations, and whitewashed break rooms with old coffee probably come to mind. It's not bad, but it certainly isn't stimulating, and in time it could be downright draining. Now imagine you work in one of WeWork's many co-working office buildings. WeWork buildings feature impeccable interior design, arcades, bars, and yes- conference rooms. These are spaces that invigorate the employee and help them do their best work. A far cry from the bland cubicle farm of the past. Silicon Valley is famous for creating spaces that nurture creativity and hard work. Look no further than workplaces like Facebook and Google to see great examples of corporations that work hard to create spaces that reflect their company values and those of their employees.

Big business has spent millions of dollars researching, and then implementing, interiors that are conducive to specific results in their employees. Learn a lesson from them and remember that your environment has the power to affect you. When you decide to manipulate your interior to be a reflection of your brand, then you will be constantly refreshed in your own purpose. I am an organized person who likes to creatively find ways to teach abstract concepts (like personal branding!) That is part of my personal brand. In my home, you'll find a mix of traditional elements mixed in creative ways that all fall into a specific order. For example, my gallery picture wall may include somewhat random elements of photos, paintings, and objects, but they are all positioned on the wall in an orderly way that brings unity. When I sit in my living room surrounded by my favorite furnishings, I feel happy and refreshed, which is exactly what a home should do.

ORGANIZE YOUR STRESS AWAY

Some people feed off of stress. They wait purposefully until the last minute because that is the moment their best work comes forth. I am not one of those people. I can operate under stress, but it isn't an ideal situation, and I certainly don't bring it upon myself. In fact, I try everything within my power to eliminate stress in any form in my life. It's this reason that I am constantly organizing my home. Look no further than the title of Marie Kondo's bestselling book *The Magic Art of Tidying Up* to see that a little organizing can go a long (even magical) distance.

There are really two types of people in the world. Those who are naturally tidy and those who are not. I am the latter, but I long to be the former. My creative streak always causes havoc in my home and is the main source of clutter. I remember inspecting a friend's immaculate room in college that was completely devoid of 'stuff' and wondering how she did it (where does she keep all her spray paint??) only to learn that she preferred reading over painting and borrowed a lot of her books. She fell into the first category. Since then, I have come to terms with the fact that I will have a little more stuff than most people, but I've also learned to organize it in a way that doesn't induce immediate anxiety. So, if you are in that latter, naturally untidy category and wishing you weren't, there is hope! Embrace who you are (it's probably the creative part of your brand) and then find a way to keep your stuff under control. Visual clutter that isn't organized gives me pretty bad anxiety, which is certainly not what I want for a relaxing home atmosphere. Here are some simple ways to beat the clutter and control your life.

1. **Put your idle time to work.** Instead of sitting on the couch during your weekly phone call with your mom/dad/sister/brother/son/daughter get up and tidy up! Walk around the house doing mindless tasks like putting away shoes, folding laundry, or dusting. It's an easy way to declutter without wasting time.

2. **Clean out your closet.** It may be a long and painful process depending on when you did it last, but the payoff is well worth it. Keeping a concise closet will save you money, hassle in the morning, and closet space. Start by taking everything (yes, everything) out of your closet. Discard anything torn or in bad condition. Donate or consign anything that you don't absolutely love. Keep only items that fit you and make you feel and look amazing. Try not to have a panic

attack at what is left. Can you believe that you've been living so long looking mediocre? Now you need to keep it clean! When you go shopping next, don't buy anything that you don't absolutely love. You deserve better than clothes that are 'fine' or 'that work'.

3. **Be a conscious consumer.** We live in a world full of mindless shopping trips, convenience buying, and retail therapy. All of these things can lead to more clutter and unnecessary items (Aka: stress) around your home. The cure is to be a conscious consumer at all times. Yes, it's annoying. Yes, it takes some time to retrain your brain and emotional responses to react differently while shopping. However, it is possible. I started doing this out of necessity when I lived in New York and had to lug any purchases home with me. There was no car to conveniently transport my superfluous shopping sprees, so I thought twice (or five times) about whether that heavy lamp, or extra can of corn, was really necessary. When you're debating a purchase, ask yourself if you really need it. Then ask yourself if you'd be willing it to carry it several city blocks along with all your other purchases. I'm willing to bet that some items will become far less important when you reflect on the immediate hassles. If you're a compulsive, award, or retail therapy shopper, start to train yourself in other ways. Use beauty treatments like pedicures and manicures as a reward instead of clothing. If you compulsively shop in order to destress or for something to do, try working out or volunteering. Your bank account and the community will thank you.

4. **Fight the inner pack rat.** You don't have to be a contender for the show Hoarders to have excess clutter negatively affect your life. Many people are naturally pack rats, and if gone unchecked, all that extra stuff has a tendency to build up into one big headache. The easiest way to battle mild hoarding is to use a two part method. First, make

frequent tidying sweeps. If you have a bad tendency to dump, this may mean walking around the house every day picking up piles of stuff from that day. If you have things a little more under control, once a week might be sufficient. Whatever you do, don't let any pile of stuff grow bigger than what you can go through in five minutes. Second, create specific dump zones and a waiting area. Dump zones may consist of two areas (maybe the front and back doors) that tend to collect the most random clutter. Place a tray or bowl in these spaces to catch all the extra stuff. When you do your daily or weekly sweeps, you'll have an automatic destination to start working through. Pack rats typically don't want to get rid of items because they may need them later. It's this reason that I suggest having a waiting area, or as I call it at home, purgatory. This may be a nice canvas drawer or wicker basket that tucks neatly into a bookshelf and holds everything that you feel you might need later. Go through your purgatory every week or every other week to either discard items that have become irrelevant (that Walgreens receipt for candy. Let's be real, you're not returning that candy) or file items that will actually be needed at a later date (that other Walgreens receipt with your HSA prescription purchase). I actually have several purgatories in my house: one for papers, one for clothing, and even one for lone socks. If I put clothes in a box, and can't tell you specifically what those items look like a month later, I clearly don't need them and they're then donated. If socks don't find their mates within the month, they're turned into cleaning rags or tossed.

MASTERING YOUR MORNING CRUNCH TIME

I don't care if you're single with no animals or have twelve kids and four dogs, mornings can be hectic. Sometimes it feels like no matter how early you wake up, chaos always ensues. Having no kids, a husband who wakes up early and takes the dog to doggy day care, and a home office, all help protect me from the morning chaos. However, my husband recently broke his knee and I've gone from laid back mornings to action packed ones filled with a mix of nurse, chauffeur, and dog duties in addition to my own work. Craziness is one word for it, but luckily, I've been able to combat the chaos with only limited side effects (which may have including things like grumbling, panic attacks, and mild crabbiness).

The secret to having a smooth morning is simple: control the things you can and let go the things you can't.

Things you can control include:

- **The time you wake up.** Sleep is great, but hitting the snooze button is going to do more harm than good. The night before, set your alarm for the latest possible time that you can get up and still have plenty of time to do what needs to be done before work. I am a night owl, yet I never used a snooze button until I got married, and clearly learned some bad habits. The sleep you get while snoozing is very low quality and unsatisfying. Do yourself the favor and tack that time onto your full night of sleep.

- **What you'll wear the next day.** Weather forecasters aren't always accurate, but they're usually correct within a general range. Check out the weather and choose your outfit accordingly so you aren't blindsided by, "Oh it's raining! I'm not sure what I'm going to wear now". If you're too tired at night to worry about tomorrow, take one day out of the week and use it to create new outfits. Get a glass of wine, or brandy, turn up the music and play dress up. Try on your clothes in different combinations and decide what outfits would work best for work, errands, or socializing. Take pictures of your favorite outfits and then reference those pictures when you're setting out your clothes the night before.

- **What you and your family will eat for breakfast**. Breakfast that is healthy and easily accessible is a winner. Bonus points if your kids can reach and prepare their own food. A well-organized pantry and refrigerator will help with this. Food options don't need to be fancy or extensive. Just having an idea of what you'll eat will take one more decision out of your morning routine. When I go grocery shopping, I usually like to buy two different breakfast options like oatmeal and granola bars. This way, I still have an option about what to eat, but neither choices are complicated or fussy. Automatic coffee machines are also wonderful things. If yours still requires the touch of a button, use it to your benefit. Fill it up the night before and teach your age appropriate children responsibility by tasking them to push the button in the morning.

- **Where important morning items are located.** There's nothing more frustrating that searching the house for your keys or phone two minutes before you need to be out the door. Create a designated spot in your house for items like this and stick with it. Key holders by the door are an obvious choice. I actually have key holders at both front and back doors and will hang my sunglasses on the same hook as my keys. When I finish using items I know I'll need to have the next day like my planner, notebooks, laptop, etc. I make an effort to immediately store them in my bag which is located next to the door. Likewise, you can have your children put their school supplies and homework back in the book bags next to the door once they have finished their homework at night. Making sure everything is in its place the night before is an easy chore for even young children. Your four year old can check to make sure the keys are on the rack (or else a game of eye spy may need to happen), while older children can be responsible for filling and placing their own backpacks in easily accessible spots.

Things you can't control include:

- **Pretty much everything else, which is okay.** You can only control so much, therefore let the rest go. Learning to roll with the punches will make you more adaptable and it often gives you some great stories (remember that time the power went out and all the ice cream melted into a giant puddle on the floor?) Whenever you feel yourself getting stressed or irritated, just remember the rule of 6's: Will you care about this incident in 6 months? What about 6 weeks? If it's not going to matter in 6 weeks or months, then it probably isn't worth worrying about.

I'm willing to bet a decent sum of money that no one filled out their personal brand statement with the words stressed, hurried, or hassled. If you don't take intentional actions to fight against stress and other negative emotions, they will naturally work their way into your life. Ask anyone what keeps them from looking their best, and they will probably reply with the excuse I hear most often, "I simply don't have enough time; I'm too busy." Just as you need to proactively work on developing a personal brand and a mission statement, you also need to work on cultivating a lifestyle that allows you effectively live out your brand. By applying the organizational and time saving tips mentioned in the last two sections, you will allow yourself more time and energy for successful personal development.

IN THE EYES OF OUR HOUSEMATES

Although there are more people living alone now than in past decades, most of us share our homes with at least one other person.

And while we are very aware of the other people around us, we don't always think about the impact our appearance makes on them. It's our home too, after all, and it's also our safe space to let down our public image.

I know what you're thinking. You're thinking that if I tell you to look perfect while fixing your kids dinner or watching TV with your roommates that you'll throw this book right out the window. Luckily for this book and whoever may be passing under your window, I'm not going to say that. It's impractical and this isn't the 1950's. The days of *Leave it to Beaver* dressing are far over.

With that said, I think it's important to think about what you look like around the house because of how it affects yourself and others. I'll start with yourself.

How do you clothe yourself when you are hanging out at home? Do you don your spouse's cast offs or do you treat yourself to luxury loungewear? Just like the way we dress at work can affect our job performance, the way we dress at home can affect our attitudes and self-esteem. Even if you're not spending a fortune, taking the extra time and money to buy clothing specifically for lounging or sleeping is a way of showing yourself respect. Instead of settling for someone else's hand me downs, you respect yourself enough to indulge in a nicer option. There are some things that you need to do just for you. These are the little things whose sole purpose is to make you happy.

I love beautiful lingerie. When I get dressed in the morning and put on a coordinating lace bra and panty set, I start the day feeling pulled together and beautiful. There are many days that my husband doesn't even see what I have on underwear wise, but that doesn't matter. I don't wear it to please him. I wear it because it makes me happy. I also shave my legs daily. I'm not one of those, 'it's the winter so I won't be shaving for two months' kind of people. Once again, this isn't something I do for anyone around me. I simply do it because I like the way my smooth legs feel when they rub against other surfaces like my pants or the bedsheets. Am I telling you to buy pretty underwear and shave your legs constantly? Of course not. The whole point is that you need to do what makes you happy. If silk nightgowns make you feel gorgeous and luxurious, then it's well worth the splurge. If going commando empowers you, then go for it! Your home is supposed to be a loving, relaxing, and refreshing place. It's hard for that to happen when you are constantly giving yourself only second best.

Then there's the other people in your home: your roommates, spouse, and/or children. Depending on your cultural upbringing you may also have extended family in your home. Cohabitating with others can be very gratifying, but it can also be a big sacrifice. You need to consider the thoughts and feelings of several other people anytime you decide to do something around the home. This not only applies to our actions, but also our presence. Our presence is a huge influence on those around us, and once this is understood, it can be a daunting reality. I'll discuss how our presence affects two of the most common housemates: our spouse and our children.

In the same way that you need to engage in grooming and dressing activities that show yourself respect and make you happy, you need to show respect to your spouse. Does this mean you have to have a full face of makeup on or be dressed in a suit and tie at the dinner table each night? Of course not. But it is nice to go the extra mile every once and while to show your spouse that you're thinking of them. If your wife has a favorite shirt of yours, make a point to wear it on date nights. Or maybe occasionally shave that beard she hates, even if you're too lazy to shave it off most days. Ladies, if your husband loves a certain dress but you think it makes you look fat, set aside your self-critique and wear it with confidence. Or, trade in your comfy underwear for something a little sexier. I promise it won't go unnoticed or unappreciated. Not only does this show the other person you care, but it is also one of the best ways to non-verbally remind them how much you love them. Mutual respect and love is essential for a lasting relationship, and both can be shown through your appearance. Remember, this is the one person that will probably look at you more times than anyone else on Earth, including yourself.

When it comes to our children, I think most parents underestimate the influence they have over their offspring. Small children hang on to your every word and movement, but the preteen and teenage years leave you wondering if you've made a mark on their lives at all. It often isn't until your children are grown with kids of their own that you start to see the impact you've made on their lives.

One of my many monthly magazine subscriptions is to Harper's Bazaar. I've read enough Bazaars to know the pattern of articles in the magazine: editor's letter, trends, fashion shoots, someone's memory of a famous person, how to stay young articles, more fashion shoots, and the occasional home and garden article. Oh yeah, and there's a celebrity expose somewhere in all that mix. One of my favorite parts of the magazine, aside from the ads, is the article that usually talks about someone's memory of another (usually famous) person. It's always interesting to hear about the life of some celebrity from decades past from the point of view of a person that knew them well. The article is almost always written in a positive, dotting tone, and the author is most often a child, niece, or close friend who essentially grew up in the household. Often times the writer fondly recalls some seemly basic activity like watching the older woman put on her lipstick or even a trivial detail like the dressing gowns worn. Even though the people profiled in these articles are almost always celebrities, we would do well to remember we are celebrities to our own children and they watch us with the same observant eyes.

Take a moment and try to imagine your daily home routine through the eyes of your child or children. What assumptions would they make about you based on what they see? How would they describe you to their friends at school? Better yet, what do you think they would write about in a Harper's Bazaar article several decades later? And, here's probably the most important question- what would you want them to write about? Remember that your personal brand isn't something you turn off when you leave the office. It should be a set of characteristics that describe your life and shape your actions. Assuming your brand is positive, they should be the key traits you wish to teach your children. It's worth taking a moment to ask yourself what kind of characteristics your kids are learning from you simply by being in your presence and observing your words and actions.

The day you said 'I do', your home transformed from a private sanctuary to a shared retreat. You traded in doing whatever you want for a mutual relationship of love and respect. When you brought home that first baby, you sacrificed even more by altering your shared retreat into a nurturing nest. You not only need to still love and respect your spouse, but you need to create an environment that is safe and supportive for children. Living with others is a delicate balance of loving yourself and respecting your housemates. An authentic personal brand is the launching point for a strong presence, and a strong presence is guaranteed to affect everyone you interact with, especially those who live with you day in and day out.

Chapter 5:
The Well Dressed Life

We've talked personal branding in general and went over the importance of your product's packaging. Then we dove into two very specific realms of life: work and home. Now we're going to zoom back out and talk about our general relationship with our appearance and how it affects our overall life. If the way you looked wasn't important, it wouldn't be a multibillion dollar industry and we'd all be walking around wearing sacks. However, what started out as a means of protection against the elements has transformed into something much more than that.

Clothing, hairstyles, and even the quality of our smile is a factor in determining status and wealth. As I stated in Chapter 2, there are specific garments for different roles in society; doctors, judges, and policemen are all set apart because of what they wear. Likewise, we can often identify prostitutes, professional swimmers, and rappers by their appearance- no uniforms needed. In fact, the contributing factor to stereotyping is image. If we all looked like little clones, stereotypes would not exist. I'm not saying that stereotypes are good, but I am saying that your image, and what it says, is important. It plays a significant role in the decisions you make and greatly influences how you are treated by others. You first need to understand the importance of your appearance before you can begin to harness it for your success. Once you respect the power of image, you can properly start using it for your gain.

THE MIND ALTERING EFFECT OF CLOTHING

People treat us differently based on our dress, but we also treat ourselves and others differently depending on what we are wearing. Have you ever put a perfectly tailored black suit on and felt on top of the world? There's a reason why it's called the power suit, after all. Maybe you help your five year old into their first basketball uniform and watch them morph into Michael Jordan. Uniforms, whether formal or informal, can give us the power to change our attitudes and alter our innate characteristics. Formal uniforms include policemen outfits, medical lab coats, and athletic jerseys. Informal uniforms are categories of dress that are defined by societal assumptions and examples include: professional suits for lawyers, skinny pants and plaid shirts for hipsters, and athletic gear for fitness instructors. We can either choose uniforms because of our career or we can adopt them depending on where we want to fit in with society.

This leads us to an issue much bigger than clothes. Where do we see ourselves in the big picture of society? If you were to say that you had no idea, you'd be lying. Whether you've cognitively made a decision about your place in society or not, you have chosen a role in the way you choose to dress yourself. Think about your daily ensembles. Think about your hair and the way you present yourself. What group or groups of people would a passing objective third party observer associate you with? After you answer that question, ask yourself who you would want to be associated with. Remember when we talked about your future goals in the personal branding chapter? What kind of person does future you look like? How is that different than the image you are currently portraying? Sometimes it helps people to work backwards. Who do you want to be in the next five, ten, twenty years? What does that person look and act like (cue: personal brand)? Now, how can you look more like that instead of who you are today? If you don't know where you're going, you'll never know how to pack for the journey. I find that many people with inconsistent images often are wandering a bit through life with very little sense of self or goals.

Figuring out where you want to be in society isn't easy. It may even takes years. But the important thing is that you try out different roles and actively seek the one that works best for you. When you find it, you'll know. As someone who was experimental with fashion all throughout middle school and high school, I remember going to Parsons School of design in New York for college and seeing all the other oddly dressed fashion lovers and thinking, 'At last! These are my people!' Your people are out there too, and believe it or not, their appearance is probably going to be one of the biggest factors drawing you to them.

When you find your people, and start dressing like your cohort in society- you will change. For one, you will grow stronger and more confident. Any suppressed desires to look a certain way will come bubbling forth. You'll feel free to 'be yourself'. You will also take on any of the traits of your group including the stereotypical ones. For example, if you enter the police academy and finally feel at home in life, your uniform will make you act a certain way. It will make you act more responsible and attentive as per your understanding of your duties, but it could also make you more aggressive and authoritative per your ingrained stereotype of police officers. An article published in the Journal of Criminology in 2012 discusses how policemen often use undressing as a method of separating their work and home life, thus keeping their home life uncontaminated from the harshness of work. This inevitably leads to the point that clothing can change us for the worse. In WWII, uniforms helped Nazis to unite and carry out atrocities, while still other uniforms were employed to completely dehumanize and kill an entire populace. This is one of the greatest examples of the psychological effect of clothing being exploited for evil purposes.

However, sometimes clothing will change you for the better. Imagine you receive a call from a coveted marketing firm asking for an interview. You can either come in now, drop in an hour later, or come two hours later. Even though you are physically close to the office now, you are wearing workout clothes from the soul cycle class you just finished. If you go to the interview now, you would feel very uncomfortable and probably perform poorly. One hour will give you just enough time to go home and put on a suit, where two hours will give you enough time to go home, shower, and put on a suit. What option are you likely to choose? My guess is the last one. You will feel and perform your best when you have a chance to look your best. We know this from experience. We've all showed up to the party wearing the wrong thing or we've seen someone else do it. Either way, we made a mental note at the time what was appropriate and what wasn't and vowed to never make that mistake again. We tend to repeat activities and experiences that give us good results, therefore, we will continue to dress well when we feel comfortable and empowered. I have certain outfits that I feel like a million dollars in, and those are the ones I repeatedly wear on stage during speaking engagements. As a result, I have a great talk and then mentally associate it with how I look, which in turn further reinforces that million dollar feeling.

The key is to find a look that resonates with your group in society and has a positive effect on both you and others. We all have a strong desire to fit in, and finding our niche in society is extremely fulfilling. Adapting dress that further allows us to fit in while also empowering us to be our best is the ultimate goal. For example, let's say that you work at a credit union. You love the family like atmosphere of your job and also the professionalism of those around you. You find several suits that you feel powerful in, and wear them as often as possible. Your confidence and strong presence then become a positive influence on your customers and coworkers. Maybe your job isn't your niche in life. That's okay. Perhaps you work at the credit union to pay the bills, but it's really your weekend Harley rides that excite you. You have several friends that get together on nice days and roll around the countryside. Your leather jacket, black boots, and helmet have the power to invigorate you and transport you elsewhere than your boring 9-5.

Wherever your special place in society is, find it! Adapt the clothing customs to fit your lifestyle and use them to empower you and encourage others. Just like putting on clothes to mimic different characters in a play, we need to find what character we want to play in the game of life and dress accordingly!

TACKLING THOSE TOUGH TRANSITION TIMES

Starting a new job. Moving to a different city. Graduating from college to the professional world. Rediscovering ourselves midlife. Ditching the work life for retirement. Our lives are full of transitional periods. It's hard enough to get through these times emotionally, let alone dress for them. However, different times call for different clothes and adjusting your wardrobe can actually help you adjust psychologically to your new role or environment.

Remember that study I mentioned in Chapter 2 about the lab coats? The researchers not only performed the initial study I talked about earlier, but also two other subsequent studies. In the second and third studies, participants were randomly assigned to wear a white lab (or doctor's) coat, a painter's coat, or had the option of having the coat hanging up in the room. Despite referring to it as either a lab or painter's coat, the coat was actually the same white coat. In both of these experiments, the participants were tested for sustained attention while they were wearing whichever clothing option they were randomly assigned. The results of the studies concluded that people wearing the white coat associated with doctors performed much better than those who were wearing street clothes, wearing a 'painter's' coat, or simply looking at the coat. The key here, is that you actually have to put the garment on and understand the symbolism associated with it, in order for the effect to be effective. If someone did not associate white coats with doctors and doctors with attentiveness, then the psychological effect would not have worked.

So what does this mean in your transition? It means that sometimes you have to wear it to become it. While the leaders of the study aren't sure whether the results were sustainable (if the participant were to wear a doctor's lab coat everyday would the boost in attentiveness wear off?) it is certain that they work in the beginning. The beginning of your transition is when you're probably going to need the most support, and if clothing can help actually change your mental abilities, then it's definitely worth a try.

If the transition is something foreseeable, start planning ahead by imagining yourself in the new role. What does 'college-graduate-professional' you look like? What about 'peak-of-your-career' you? How about 'retired-and-relaxed' you? For whatever scenario you are faced with, think about what you would be doing, what you will be wearing, and how you want to be perceived. Then start thinking about how your appearance needs to change to fit into that image. This may mean buying one nice professional garment each month the year before you graduate in order to have a functioning, work appropriate wardrobe post collegiate. Maybe it means reassessing your everyday business casual work clothes and switching them out for the more professional, sleek suits of the high power jobs you want your career to move towards. Perhaps you need to go the opposite direction and start focusing on living a more low maintenance lifestyle to prepare yourself for retirement. The sooner you start figuring out the needs and goals of future you, the quicker present day you can start transitioning into that role.

If possible, step into that new role as often as possible before it starts. Even if there isn't a start date, you can still start acting like the person you would like to be. A middle management employee hoping to rise to upper management can start the transition to their upper management self by physically appearing and actively acting the part. This shows your employer that, while you are excelling at your current position, you are ready and capable to take it to the next level. Just like the professors at Northwestern found, if you begin to dress the role you want, you will begin to display characteristics of that position which makes you more confident and makes others view you as more capable.

Transition isn't always planned, however, and even if it is, we aren't always prepared. A new job, relocation, or career change can leave us feeling ill equipped for our new environment. The key is to avoid panicking and funnel that energy into something useful- like creating an action plan. Figure out what brand packaging your new role requires and then assess your current packaging (or your current image). Identify the gaps and then figure out a short term and long term action plan to help you bridge that gap. This is something I do all the time for my image consulting clients. Here's a great example of this method at work:
Jackie was recently let go from her position in billing at a local medical facility. Tired of behind the scenes work, she decides to make a bold move and put her sales skills to work as a realtor. Having always had a love for real estate and a likable personality, she becomes a licensed realtor. Jackie is excited about her new job, but she learns quickly

that the jeans and cardigan sets of her previous job aren't going to work in real estate. The first thing she does is decides who the ideal realtor Jackie looks like. Next, she brainstorms ways that she can achieve aspects of that image, without spending too much time or money. Maybe she keeps the sweater sets and pairs them with dress pants. Perhaps she finds some professional clothing second hand, she in unemployed after all, but splurges on an up to date haircut. Jackie then creates long term goal likes creating a complete professional wardrobe, updating her accessories, and upgrading her car. Now, what seemed like an impossible task has been broken down into manageable parts with instant gratification.

No matter if you are going through a planned or unforeseen transition, these times can be difficult. To make it easier, have a clear idea of your personal brand and the person you are becoming. Once you understand the person you are outfitting and break down the process into bite size pieces, you will be one step closer to gaining the confidence you need and ruling your new position!

WHO ARE YOU REALLY DRESSING FOR?

We all walk a fine line of being true to ourselves and also trying to please others. Sometimes we can do both and sometimes we can't, but I think that's exactly where we should be...right on the line. Many of us have been entirely in one camp or the other and can probably relate to my story of finding the perfect equilibrium.

When I was in middle school, specifically sixth and seventh grade, I wanted to be like every other preteen girl and fit in. I didn't even necessarily want to be the cool kid. I was totally okay with mediocrity as long as I wasn't dubbed a loser. I shopped in all the right places and had a whole fleet of butterfly clips for my hair (hello 90's). I was way too shy to be cool, but I was okay with that. I had no clue who I was and I wasn't ready to be the cool kid that got to make all the decisions (Becky is so lame, don't you think?) At the same time, I was trying to figure out what I liked and what I didn't. In essence, I was figuring out who I was.

At the beginning of my eighth grade year I had an epiphany. Or at least as much of an epiphany as a 13 year old is capable of having. Are you ready for it? It was pretty meaty: I shouldn't care what other people think. Yeah, that was it. It seems so simple, but it's a concept that some adults still struggle to grasp. In that eighth grade year I felt free. I ditched the clothes that I wore because they were cool, but didn't necessarily like and started experimenting with fashion. The next two years would involve lots of really bad sartorial decisions including, but not limited to, sequin cowboy hats, rainbow toe socks, and cow print bandanas. High school refined my taste, but it was still pretty out there. Four inch heels and miniskirts were regular occurrences as was ocean washed hair from early morning surf sessions.

My 'I do what I want' fashion tirade ended very vainly my freshman year in college. I looked over at a fellow student in English 101 and was immediately taken aback by her thigh cellulite. She was tall, thin and wearing a mini skirt. And she had cellulite. I almost died. Do I have cellulite? I didn't even know that could happen to thin people. My legs were by far my best attribute and miniskirts were my thing. I went back to my dorm immediately after class and sat down in front of the mirror. Sure enough, the thighs dimpled. I think I boxed up every mini skirt I owned and drove right to Goodwill. It was just after I swore I would never be that girl that I realized how much I truly did actually care what people thought of me. Was it vain that I freaked out over a little cellulite? Absolutely. Am I proud of my thoughts and actions? Not particularly. While that story is mildly embarrassing and extremely shallow, it was the turning point of how I assessed other's opinions of me. It was also the start of a long journey to find a balance between staying true to myself and weighing the opinions of others.

From that day to this one, I've been testing the boat of caring and not caring about other's opinions of my appearance. Some days I just really want to wear an avant garde outfit, which is always met with raised eyebrows in my Iowan city. Other days I strategically dress specifically for the encounter I'm about to have. The key to finding a happy medium is to respect both sides of the playing field. Respect your own wishes, desires, and personality. However, also respect others. Respect their cultures, beliefs, and opinions of you. You won't be able to please everyone, but it is possible to respectful of most parties present- including yourself.

RESPECT THE WELL-EARNED DOLLAR

It's hard to talk about changing your appearance without broaching the subject of money. Fiscal restrictions are some of the top excuses people give when telling me about their wardrobe woes. One would almost be led to believe that money can solve all image issues. That is, unless one actually had the joy of witnessing many people with money royally mess up their appearance. The point is, you don't have to have a million dollars to look a million dollars. Rather, you have to know how to spend what you have wisely. In this chapter, we'll work through some of the most commonly believed myths I see my clients struggle with.

Myth 1: Expensive labels make you look better.

This statement is both true and false. Designer clothing tends to be better made. For that reason, a Ralph Lauren Black Label pant will fit you better than a Forever 21 pant. That's pretty obvious, and it's about where things end. Even if the construction of the garment is better, if it doesn't fit you well, it will still make you look bad. An altered to fit Banana Republic jacket will look better than an off the rack Armani number that was made to fit the general populous, but not you specifically. Clothes that fit and flatter you will look better than ones that don't, no matter the price point. Period. Logos also won't make you look better. An armful of Gucci print products might make you friends in some arenas, but in others it will mark you as shallow and vying for attention. If you genuinely love the print, that's one thing. If you find yourself pining after a product just because you want to show off the labels, you will come across as shallow and insecure, and that doesn't look good on anyone.

Myth 2: More is more.

Sometimes it's better to have more stuff, but most of the time it isn't. If you're trying to make a statement, then layering five necklaces might be a good idea. If you feel the need to have a closet the size of a shopping mall because you define your value in quantity, that's not great. With today's fast fashion, it's so easy to purchase a million items for very little at your local H&M or Zara. If that's a good idea for you, or not, depends on why you are buying. If you're doing it as retail therapy or because you're trying to keep up with the Jones', you'll never be happy. If you're doing it because you genuinely love experimenting with fashion, need lots of options for your career, or see it as a form of art- have at it. Collecting clothing for the latter reasons is much healthier than using shopping as an emotional Band-Aid or to keep up appearances.

Myth 3: Quantity over Quality

This is another yes and no scenario. There are some articles of clothing- coats, blazers, tailored pants, and a classic dress- that the rule of *quality over quantity* should apply to. I own very few of the aforementioned items, but they are the nicest versions that I can afford. On the other hand, you have clothing where the 'quality above all' rule doesn't exist. Shirts are one of those things for me. This is because I work my clothing hard, and I am a dirty person. Oil and red wine seem to find me wherever I go. I never buy a white shirt full price. Or white pants for that matter. In fact, at the end of every summer, I buy a new pair of white jeans from Old Navy or Gap to replace the ones I've ruined the previous year (pollen was the main saboteur this year). Could I buy a much nicer pair of jeans? Of course. But since I know they'll only last a season, it isn't worth it. I'd rather save my money for those classic items that tend to weather the storm a bit better.

Myth 4: If you want to look nice, you need to spend more money

It is very possible to look classy while on a shoestring budget. College students in particular often cite limited finances as a reason to looking less than their best. As a result, I always make sure to add a 'dressing on a budget' portion to my college lectures. The key to looking like you spent more money than you did is to choose classic silhouettes in neutral colors. Bright, trendy clothing reads as cheap, while neutral, classic shapes read as more expensive and classy. Even if you shop nowhere but Forever 21, you can still look polished, by buying neutral colors and classic shapes (think: sheath dress, button down shirt, boot cut dress pants). Likewise, doing your own nails and coloring your own hair can be inexpensive and effective ways to look better without the extra expense.

Myth 5: It needs to be all or nothing

This is the one myth that I find people commonly act out much more than they verbally confess. It can manifest itself in one of two ways. The first way is on an item by item basis. "If I can't afford XYZ mascara from Sephora, then I won't wear any". Once again, it usually doesn't play out verbally like that. Instead, you run out of makeup and then choose to wait until your next paycheck rather than buy Maybelline to hold you over. The second way the 'all or nothing' mindset works, is by our whole image. You know people that always look perfect or look absolutely rough, right? That's who I'm talking about. You see this a lot in guys who rebel from their work week attire of suits to cargo shorts and band t-shirts with seemingly no in between ensembles. Both methods of 'all or nothing' are bad because they allow us to fall short of looking our best at all times. Like I stated previously, you don't have to wear a suit at all times, but your brand image should be consistent no matter where you are or what you're doing. Sometimes this means forking over some chump change for mascara that isn't 'your brand' or running the risk of looking great and having no one see.

You work hard for your money and you want to make sure it's well spent. Spending money on your image is necessary, but the amount you spend will depend on the image you want to portray and your general lifestyle. Remember our box of cookies from way back in chapter 1? In order to sell those cookies, you absolutely needed something to package them in. The price of your packaging will differ depending on how snazzy, simple, or complex it is. The design, and also the price, will change depending on the image you want convey to your consumer. Likewise, the packaging on your brand (i.e.: your image) will vary in price depending on the image you want to portray. It may take a couple of test runs to identify the best places to spend your money (an expensive hair treatment may be much better spent than designer clothing), but once you find the right formula, you will start seeing immediate results.

Chapter 6:
Don't just sit there

If there's one thing I hate, it's a goal without a plan. A great idea with no actionable items to bring it into reality is a waste. Hopefully, you have been inspired in this book to seek out your personal brand and start working on your brand packaging. Or maybe a particular chapter resonated with you and made you start thinking about change. Whatever the case, I want to help you tackle the daunting task of improving your personal brand and its image. When broken down into easy to do checklists, changing your appearance becomes easier than you ever imagined.

Because different people approach change in different ways, I've provided two different types of action plans: Plan A-ll together now and Plan B-ut let's do it one at a time. Plan A-ll together now is for people who like a simple guide to jump in and tackle the whole issue head on, while Plan B-ut let's do it one at a time is catered towards individuals who are more comfortable with bite size pieces and more direction. Both plans will result in the same place, but the time frame and depth will vary.

PLAN A-LL TOGETHER NOW

If your favorite pool dive as a child was a cannonball, this action plan is for you. Designed to go head first into self-examination and potential change, this option is for the go getters. This action plan is also a bit more general. If you would prefer a more detailed plan, see Plan B. While I have split these activities into four weeks, you can alter the schedule to fit your personal needs.

Week 1: Discover your personal brand

Spend this first week really getting to know yourself and your goals. Start by filling out the Personal Branding Exercise at the end of Chapter 1.

Goal: By the end of week one, you should have a strong personal brand statement and mission statement.

Week 2: Assess your work image

Spend this week getting feedback from coworkers and friends about your appearance and body language. Figure out what parts of your image are adding to your success at work and which aren't. Make changes as necessary. The Body Language Exercise at the end of Chapter 2 will help in this process. (Alternatively, you can hire an image consultant either in person, or online* to help you objectively assess your image and provide feedback.)

Goal: Know your weaknesses and your strengths when it comes to your appearance. Start creating a list of items to improve upon.

Week 3: Organize your home life

Anytime you're at home this week and are stressed, upset, or acting differently than how you wish to be known, take a brief moment to write down what the source of the problem is. Are you angry about misplaced keys or dirty clothes? Did you trip over little Jimmy's shoes for the fourth time this week? Does your closet produce never ending bouts of anxiety when you get ready each day? At the end of the week, review your list and look for patterns. Put actions in place to prevent the same aggravators from reappearing again. Then, create an action plan to cope with stress that isn't controllable (ideas include: exercise, meditation, painting, etc.)

Goal: Know what your biggest home enemies are and have a list of ways to tackle them throughout the coming weeks.

Week 4: Take action

At this point you should have several lists including, who you are and what your goals are, body language and appearance improvements, and home improvements. Looking back over your mission statement, decide which improvements will impact your goals most. Your closet may be in a sad state of affairs, but it's your constant negative body language that is stunting your career. I recommend ranking your improvement items and then taking a week to focus on each one, most important first.

Goal: By the end of the month, you should have a complete action plan to start looking the way you want to be perceived...now follow it!

*If the thought of objectively analyzing your appearance and body language seems impossible, then an Image Consultant may be helpful. Image Consultants are trained to help people, just like you, look the way they want to be perceived. You can find an Image Consultant by searching the AICI (American Image Consultants International) website or simply typing in Image Consultant + [your city] into your preferred web search engine. If the idea of web based consultation makes you feel more comfortable, my Image Consulting Company provides personalized advice straight to your inbox. All you have to do, is purchase a package online, fill out a brief survey and snap a few pictures. Then, within a week, you'll receive your personalized report via email. For more information see: **http://leslie-friedman.com/about/**

PLAN B-UT LET'S DO IT ONE AT A TIME:

If you're the kid at the pool that likes to dip their toe in before they jump (or slowly wade), this action plan is for you. Maybe you lead a busy life and don't have the time and energy to do everything at once. Maybe it's too overwhelming. Whatever the reason, this action plan is spread out over a longer period of time to be more digestible. I have also gone more in depth with Plan B, for those who like to have guidance every step of the way. While I have split this process over the course of 4 months, you can alter the schedule to fit your lifestyle. I recommend using a notebook to make notes and keep them easily accessible.

Month 1: Discover your personal brand

Week 1: Start collecting a list of people you admire. These could be friends, family members, coworkers, or Fortune 500 billionaires. Next to each name on your list, write down characteristics about that person that you admire.

Week 2: Now start dreaming big. What kind of person do you want to be in the future? What does future you's lifestyle look like? What do people say about future you? If you're having trouble with this activity, just pretend that you're reading your own obituary. What would you want it to say? Now, do some research about people that currently hold your dream position. What characteristics do they have? How do they act and dress? How would you describe their personal brands?

Week 3: Ask friends, coworkers, and acquaintances to give you objective opinions about what they think your brand is. An easy way to do this is to send out a google form asking them to describe you in five words. This is a completely anonymous way to collect and analyze information without making people uncomfortable or jeopardizing friendships. Once you collect the data, look for any trends. The Personal Branding Exercise at the end of Chapter 1 may also be useful in helping you or someone else brainstorm your strongest characteristics.

Week 4: Figure out what you're doing well and what you aren't.* Make three columns. On the far left column, write down the most common attributes of people you admire/person in your dream job. In the middle column write down the attributes, or personal brand, that you would like to be known for. In the last column, write down the descriptors your survey generated. Look for the similarities. These are going to be the strong parts of your brand or the things you are doing well. Also look for any contrasting descriptors. Inconsistencies mean that your brand isn't streamlined. Even if the inconsistencies are still good words, if they aren't the words (or at least similar to the words) that you'd like to be known by, then they aren't helping build a strong brand.

Next, take everything you've learned about yourself and the person you want to be and use the formula in Chapter 1 to create a personal brand statement and a mission statement. Display these statements somewhere you'll see them every day. This will help keep you on track and focused.

Goal: By the end of month 1, you should have a well-defined personal brand statement and mission statement.

Month 2: Assess your work image

Week 1: Assess how you're being perceived at work. If you surveyed your coworkers in the last month, review the survey. Did they think you were professional or sloppy? Did they think you were likely to cut corners or were detail oriented? If you can, try to figure out on your own why these assumptions were made. Alternatively, you could ask an honest friend, a coworker, or an image consultant to help you identify what in your appearance is making others see you a certain way.

Week 2: Take a minute to analyse your industry, company, and job position. How do people in your position or your industry typically look? How do they act? Now, try to pinpoint several people in your field who are particularly successful. What do they do that isn't like everyone else? How do they act? What do they wear? How do they move and what body language do they use?

Week 3: Compare your actions and appearance to those who are more successful than you in your industry. Make a list of differences (ex. Always dresses nicer than most people, uses confident body language, etc.) and then decide if improving on these points will help you reach your end goal. For example, the successful person may laugh a lot and you do not. If you feel that being serious is part of your personal brand, you may choose to not bridge that gap. Remember, that the people you are admiring have their own quirks and personalities. You are not trying to copy everything that person does (I'm sure the successful person you are emulating would think it's weird if you went around copying their laugh), but use any tactics they are using to also get ahead. The body language exercise at the end of Chapter 2 provides a good template for helping you analyse others and create goals.

Week 4: Now that you've identified some points to work on, make an action plan. What are you going to do in the next couple weeks to improve your appearance and body language? Maybe you decide that every weekend for a month, you'll go through your closet and start editing anything that doesn't fit with your brand. Maybe you'll buy one professional piece of clothing a month. Or perhaps, you'll choose an aspect of body language to focus on each week for a specific amount of time (ex. Week 1- smiling and appearing more friendly, week 2- not fidgeting, week 3- sitting up straight, etc.). Remember, the more manageable your goals are the more likely you are to achieve them. You'll also be more likely to achieve them if you engage others. Tell friends, family, and coworkers what you're working on and have them help keep you accountable.

Goal: By the end of month 2, you should have a clear understanding of how you are viewed at work and have a realistic action plan to bridge any gaps between how you're currently being perceived and your ideal personal brand.

Month 3: Organize your home life

Week 1: Anytime you're at home this week and are stressed, upset, or acting differently than how you wish to be known, take a brief moment to write down what the source of the problem is. Is your closet such a mess that it leaves you with ever growing anxiety? Do you not leave yourself enough time in the morning to get ready and always feel rushed? Would you rather gouge your eyeballs out than run a specific errand? Whatever it is, write it down and then look for similarities. Also note which things can be prevented and which can't.

Week 2: Use this week to actively work on the things from your list that can prevented. Maybe you negotiate with your husband so he runs the errand you hate and you take one of his less preferred chores. Perhaps you start to organize the closet that is driving you crazy. Whatever it is, set a plan in place to tackle the source of your preventable stress.

Week 3: There are some stressors that are just unavoidable and, often times, when it rains it pours. If you don't already have a go-to stress relief activity, spend this week experimenting with ways to maintain your stress when those less than perfect days hit. Try taking a yoga class, pick up an adult coloring book, or learn new breathing techniques. When you find something you like, stick with it. These hobbies will become your 'quiet, you time' during the week and will help re-energize you. It's always good to have a couple of methods for different occasions. Your go to relaxation activity of rock climbing may not be plausible at work when you get freaked out, but taking a moment to practice deep breathing is perfectly acceptable.

Week 4: You've identified (and hopefully) taken action on some potential preventable stressors this month. You've also worked on ways to deal with issues you cannot control. Now it is time to really reflect on your personal brand at home. What kind of spouse, parent, roommate, or friend are you? Would those who live with you and know you best describe you as your personal brand statement? Is your mission statement apparent to them? Share with your loved ones your branding goals and your life goals that you've been developing. Don't be afraid to ask for their feedback and to ask for their help in achieving your dreams. With that said, remember that family is a two way street. Be sure to ask how you can also help them achieve their personal best!

Goal: Identify possible stressors and have a game plan for keeping them in control.

Month 4: Making a lasting plan

Week 1: You've been working on a lot over the past few months. Take a moment to review all your improvement plans and goals you've made over the past three months. Create a reasonable action plan that works best for you. Don't be disheartened if your plan spreads over the course of several months or even a year. It may be easier to focus on one major change a month for a year than to try to tackle twelve things at once.

Week 2: Here's the fun part of goal setting: once you make the aforementioned plan, set up rewards for yourself. Rewards can be anything you chose from a new dress to a box of cookies. Keep in mind though, that successful people use every card given to them and choosing your own rewards is just another card. So, perhaps you choose treating yourself to a full day of golf when you achieve a goal. While golf is something you enjoy, it may also be a good skill to know when you're schmoozing with the CEO during the annual company golf outing. Likewise, treating yourself to a manicure when you reach a goal is not only pleasant for you, but it also makes you look more polished and professional. The important thing is to choose rewards that excite you and really help you stay on track to meet your goals.

Ongoing: Always be open to ongoing feedback. This is the easiest way to know if your personal brand is accurate and that you are truly living out your mission statement. Feedback might be informal, such as coworker introducing you in a new way that is representative of the brand you've been working on building (e.g. "This is Sam, he's the most compassionate and helpful person you'll ever meet") or simply telling you that they've noticed a difference. It may also be formal, as in the form of a raise or promotion at work. Those, of course, are examples of unsolicited feedback. As long as you are being courteous to others, you can also gather solicited feedback every so often. This may involve going to a friend, family member, or coworker and asking about something specific you've been working on. For example, you might ask a coworker what they think of your new professional outfit. Or you might ask a friend whether they've noticed a difference in your posture.

As I mentioned in Chapter 1, developing and maintaining a personal brand isn't something you do once and never again. As you change, your priorities, values, and goals will change also. It's important to periodically reassess your brand and be receptive to feedback as it ensures your brand and goals are growing along with you.

*If the thought of objectively analyzing your appearance and body language seems impossible, then hiring an Image Consultant may be helpful. Image Consultants are trained to help people, just like you, look the way they want to be perceived. You can find an Image Consultant by searching the AICI (American Image Consultants International) website or simply typing in Image Consultant + [your city]. If the idea of web based consultation makes you feel more comfortable, my Image Consulting Company provides personalized advice straight to your inbox. **Visit** http://leslie-friedman.com **or email Leslie at** empowerme@leslie-friedman.com **for more information.**

Conclusion

What do Michael Jordan, Malala Yousafzai, and Mindy Kaling all have in common? They figured out what makes them unique and then put it to work living out their mission statements. As a result, the personal brands they created become household names across America and, in some cases, the entire world. Each of these individuals also mastered the power of dress to effectively support their goals. They were able to leverage the cards dealt them to improve their own lives and the lives of those around them. Here's the big thing about personal branding: it's not just about you. Sure, this entire book is about how to improve your life and make you more successful, but your sole wellbeing is not my end goal with this publication. My end goal is to inspire you to live such full, purposeful lives that everyone you encounter is positively influenced by your presence. My hope is that, in developing a strong personal brand and life mission, that you would not merely be an observer in this world, but a positive change agent. Within each of us is an incredible power to change the lives of those around us. Tap into that power, and you'll not only help yourself, but you'll help the world.

Imagine that you are an African American girl born to a single mother in the Deep South just before the Civil Rights movement. Your teen mother abandons you with her mother just after you're born and you spend the first several years of your life in extreme poverty. You have an obscure biblical name no one can pronounce and your often don clothing made from potato sacks. The next decade of your life is filled with sexual abuse from family members, an unstable home life, and a still born baby born when you are just 14.

Unfortunately, the life you are imaging is the background of a real woman. Despite an upbringing that would crush anyone's spirits, this young woman stayed in high school and, unknowingly, started identifying her personal brand. She was smart, and she could talk- a talent that won an oratorical contest with college tuition as the prize. Her quick wit and public speaking skills, both key components of her brand, landed her a job after college working in television. Today, Oprah Winfrey's net worth is 3.2 billion dollars and she has been called "one of the most influential women in the world" by multiple sources including TIME magazine.

When Oprah came into this world, she didn't come with a full deck of cards. However, she used what she had and cultivated an empire. If you look at everything Oprah has produced in her adult life, you will see similar themes of inspiration, empowerment, and philanthropy. These are the common threads that are the foundation of her personal brand. Whether you look at her giving record (she was the first African American to rank among the 50 most generous Americans), her film career (starting with The Color Purple), or her own talk show, Oprah has found a way to infuse her brand in everything she does. In the process, she has not only made herself wildly successful in terms of fame and money, but she has also helps millions along the way.

Whether you were born to a teen mom in rural Mississippi like Oprah, or were born with a silver spoon, you have character traits that make you uniquely you. Develop those traits, establish goals, and start looking and acting like the very best version of you. It's that version that will lead you to a successful life and, hopefully, lift up others along the way.

About the Author

Through a unique blend of personal branding and image consulting strategies, Leslie Friedman is helping people all over the world gain confidence and seize the success they deserve.

As an Image Consultant and Professional Speaker, Leslie travels the globe empowering others. Unlike most Image Consultants, who only alter your outward appearance to be more up to date or trendy, Leslie works from the inside out, helping clients and audiences to discover their personal brand and then dress (fabulously, of course!) for the brand they want to portray to the world. This inside out approach to image control sets the recipient up for prolonged, effective success rather than offering a fashion band-aid and Leslie has seen its lasting power on individual clients and large audiences alike._All Leslie's services are available online through her website, which makes them easily accessible to busy individuals regardless of location.

Leslie attended the University of Georgia and Parsons School of Design for Fashion Merchandising and Fashion Design, respectively. After school, she spent almost a decade designing women's clothing while managing everything from department stores to small start-ups. After years of retail experience, working directly with customers, and opportunities putting on fashion events, Leslie realized that most women struggle with their appearance in various ways. This could be anything from shopping, to putting outfits together, to dressing properly for work. She also noticed that, unless you drive to the next metropolis, smaller communities don't have access to Image Consultants to help them with these issues. Additionally, no matter if you're in an urban area or rural, Leslie noticed that many Image Consultants simply worked to make their clients beautiful for today, rather than focusing on how to change the appearance of the person to ensure long term success. The combination of these factors, along with a strong drive to help others, led Leslie to establish an Image Consulting business that is based in the concept of personal branding. Always a teacher at heart, Leslie's goal is to teach lifelong lessons that anyone can apply at any age in order to take control of their appearance and enhance their life.

Leslie lives in Elberton, Georgia with her husband and three animals: Coco, Jacques, and Pierre. When she isn't helping others, Leslie enjoys running, ballet, volunteering, reading non-fiction books, and watching way too much HGTV.

Connect with Leslie:

Website: **www.leslie-friedman.com**

Email: **empowerme@lesliefriedman.com**

Facebook: **https://www.facebook.com/friedmanleslie/**

Twitter: **@FriedmanTalks**

Special Thanks...

To my parents who raised me to stay true to myself and follow my dreams ("you can be whatever you want...as long as it pays the bills!")

To my sisters, who encouraged me rather than made fun of me, when I said I was going to write a book.

To my husband, who has supported me every (late night typing session) minute of the way.

To my dog, cat, and chinchilla, who respectively annoy me, love me, and amuse me on a daily basis.

To my clients, who continue to enrich my life and teach me new things every day.

To Henry Jagush, who was concerned he wouldn't be mentioned in this book. I saved the last line for you.

www.ingramcontent.com/pod-product-compliance
Lightning Source LLC
Chambersburg PA
CBHW021431170526
45164CB00001B/196